MAGIC TRICKS
&
CARD TRICKS

Two Books Bound as One

By Wilfrid Jonson
Edited by Chesley V. Barnes

Dover Publications, Inc., New York

This Dover edition, first published in 1954, is a
revised republication of two works by Wilfrid Jonson
originally published in 1950 under the titles
Conjuring and *Card Conjuring*. These works are
reprinted by special arrangement with W. & G.
Foyle, Ltd., publisher of the original editions.

International Standard Book Number: 0-486-20909-1
Library of Congress Catalog Card Number: 53-10031
Manufactured in the United States of America

Dover Publications, Inc.
180 Varick Street
New York, N. Y. 10014

MAGIC TRICKS

By
Wilfrid Jonson

Edited by Chesley V. Barnes

Dover Publications, Inc., New York

CONTENTS

PREFACE

To condense the Art of Conjuring, the subject of a thousand books, into one Handbook of this length, is plainly impossible even to a conjurer. One can only give a representative selection from the best feats of modern conjuring to illustrate as many as possible of the basic principles of the art. That, indeed, was the purpose of the publishers: to provide a " first book of conjuring " which would give the reader a repertoire of tricks for amateur performance and provide a possible stepping stone to greater things.

When the Author first started conjuring there were not many books and these few were not very helpful to beginners. They demanded that the student should spend long weary hours learning intricate and difficult sleight-of-hand movements and spend considerable sums on elaborate equipment. The reader of this Handbook will be expected to possess neither inexhaustible patience and perseverance nor a bottomless purse. The equipment he will need will be little and inexpensive and the amount of sleight-of-hand he will be asked to learn, he will be able to acquire in a very limited period.

The curious processes used by the conjurer are not always easy to describe and we have not hesitated to sacrifice style to clarity of technical explanation when we thought it necessary. At times our descriptions may appear to be too detailed, but these details should be carefully studied, for successful conjuring is mainly a matter of giving great attention to the smallest points. Genius is said to be an infinite capacity for taking pains and it is certain that, in this business of conjuring, there is much truth in the saying. We must ask you, therefore, to read our descriptions with care, for we have supplemented them by the smallest possible number of illustrations, believing

7

that it is only an inattentive reader and an incompetent author who require batteries of drawings to amplify the text: as French writers on conjuring have always maintained.

You will learn the general principles of magic better by studying specific tricks than by reading long essays upon the subject, but a few observations regarding your approach and general attitude to the matter will not be out of place. First, you should remember that the object of a conjurer is not, *primarily* to deceive. That is his secondary object—his first being to *entertain*. So you will avoid presenting your tricks with an air of challenge and you will avoid also an air of superiority. You can best do this by appearing a little amused and puzzled by the effects you produce, by appearing to be conducting experiments in an art which you have not altogether mastered and which still, at times, astonishes you.

A second thing to remember is that you cease to be a conjurer when you have finished your performance. Nothing can be more irritating to really intelligent people than the conjurer who poses as a " magician " and pretends to be a man of mystery *after* he has finished his act. The Author hopes that you will become a conjurer but not a conjuring bore.

WILFRID JONSON.

London, 1949.

PART 1

IMPROMPTU

THERE is good reason to believe that conjuring has been practised since pre-historic times: it is certain that the world's oldest conjuring trick, The Cups and Balls, has been known since the dawn of civilization. Even if we set aside the dubious evidence of an Egyptian wall painting, and the vague testimony of a Greek vase, we find written descriptions of the trick in early Roman literature which show that even then it was an old and much developed feat of legerdemain.

But this is not the place to write a history of conjuring: our aim is to show you how to take your place in the long line of conjurers who have practised and developed the art from its early primitive stage to its present extensive cultivation. For that you need but two things, intelligence and perseverance. We regret the necessity for the latter but, although we shall do our best to smooth away your difficulties, a certain amount of diligence will still be indispensable.

Most books on conjuring begin by asking the student to learn a multitude of " sleights " before he is shown how to do any " tricks." We shall avoid this tedious method and teach you the sleights as, and when, you need them in the performance of tricks. Only by doing tricks can you learn to be a conjurer, and the sooner you start doing them, the better. The first part of the Handbook will therefore be given over to Impromptu Tricks with common objects which you can do at a moment's notice for the amusement of your friends. The second part will be devoted to tricks which can form a place in a set programme when you have advanced sufficiently to give a complete performance.

It is commonly supposed that the conjurer needs great dexterity and it is true that at times he exhibits very considerable skill, but his skill generally lies, not so much

9

in the quickness, as in the precision of his movements, in the *timing* of his actions. The trick that follows will illustrate our meaning:

THE COIN THROUGH THE HAND

A coin passes through the back of the conjurer's hand.

We must ask you always to read our instructions with the simple properties required, in this case only a quarter or a half-dollar, in your hands, and to follow our directions carefully and, at first, slowly, until you understand them thoroughly. Proceed step by step and master each point as you go and you will greatly simplify the labour of learning.

With the half-dollar held in the right hand at the tips of the fingers and thumb, close your left hand into a fist and hold it in front of you, breast high, back uppermost. Tap the edge of the coin on the back of the hand . . . once . . . twice . . . and at the third time allow the coin to slide behind the fingers so that they hide it from the view of persons standing in front of you. It will then be held flat against the two middle fingers by a slight pressure of the thumb. Keeping the right hand quite still, turn the left hand over, and open it, as if you had suddenly remembered that you had not shown that hand empty at the beginning. Then turn the hand back to its previous closed position and, as you do so, allow the coin to slip from behind the right fingers inside the left hand, by slightly releasing the pressure of the right thumb. The appearance of the two hands remains as before. There is nothing to show an onlooker that the coin is not still behind the fingers of the right hand, resting on the back of the left hand. Now move the position of the right fingers as though you were placing the coin *flat* on the back of the hand and then, with a little rubbing movement, pretend to push the coin right through the hand. Turn the left hand and open it to show the coin inside.

Let us summarize. Close the left hand, tap the coin on its back, and let the coin slide behind the right fingers, which hide it. Open the left hand and show it empty and, as you again close it, let the coin drop from behind the right fingers into the left hand. Finally, pretend to rub the coin through the back of the hand.

Stand before a mirror (which shall be your first " audience " and will let you see yourself as others will later see you when you attempt to do the trick to friends) and go over all these movements again.

You will see at once that, to obtain a good illusion the *timing* of the trick must be perfect. The coin must be dropped just at the moment when the edge of the left hand, in its turning movement, passes just below the tips of the right fingers. This is the part of the trick you must assiduously practise and you must not attempt to show it even to your best friend until you have thoroughly mastered it.

Perhaps you have realised by now that to make the trick a pleasant little comedy you will need to act it out a bit and I will here tell you the true secret of conjuring. *The real* secret of conjuring is *ACTING*. In your first efforts try to imagine that you are really doing what you pretend to do, that is to say, imagine that you are really rubbing the coin through the back of your hand by means of some magic power. Let your imagination direct your actions so that later you can act as if you were really doing what you say you do. There are some conjurers who perform with such ease, and act so well, that, watching them, one forgets that " there is a trick in it " and is content to marvel. It is then that conjuring has a right to be called " magic."

In addition to Timing, two other principles of conjuring were illustrated by the little trick we have just discussed: *Simulation* and *Afterthought*. After the coin had been dropped into the left hand the right fingers were held as though they still contained it, *simulating* the presence of the coin in the right hand. The principle is very widely used and you will employ it often. The *Afterthought* also is often used. You will remember that at the beginning of the trick you very conveniently " forgot " to show your left hand empty. This gave you an excuse to open it at the opportune moment. It is obvious however, that if you were to repeat the trick, immediately, to the same spectators, you would have no excuse for once more forgetting to show the hand at the start. This brings us to one of the accepted rules of conjuring. *Never repeat a trick to the same audience unless a considerable interval of time has elapsed or you can perform it by some other method.* It is not that every trick has an afterthought but that every *good* trick has an element of surprise which is its most effective point, and that all surprises are less astonishing when they are repeated. In addition, all tricks are much more difficult to perform successfully when the spectators know what to expect and are more on their guard at the critical moments.

The following excellent impromptu, for forty years a favourite trick of many first rate conjurers, illustrates the same principles.

THE WANDERING COINS

Four coins travel invisibly to join each other.

You require four coins (quarters or half-dollars, as nearly alike as possible) a large handkerchief or a table napkin, and two playing cards, pieces of paper, or envelopes; two used envelopes from your pocket, containing letters, will do admirably. You spread the napkin on the table and place a coin at each corner, A, B, C, D, thus:

A   B

D   C

You then toss the two envelopes down on the table so that they cover the two coins D and B, and you tell your audience a story something like this:

" This is an old Chinese mystery with four coins, two of which must always be visible and two invisible. All sorts of combinations can be made, but always two coins must be visible and two invisible." As you say this you pick up the envelopes and, holding one in each hand, you shift them about so that they cover, successively, coins A and B, A and D, B and C and C and D. The exact order in which you cover the coins is not important provided you make up a definite order and stick to it, so that you can make all the movements rapidly and without hesitation, *while you are talking.*

Naturally you will hold the envelopes with your thumbs on top and your fingers underneath and, as you cover coins C and D, the right second finger nail is slipped beneath coin C and the coin is quietly picked up beneath the envelope. At the same moment the left hand, bearing its envelope, moves just in front of the right hand, and as the right hand moves away with coin C beneath the envelope, the left hand drops the other envelope on to the space vacated. The right hand passes on to cover, momentarily, with its envelope, first, coin D, and then coin B, and the envelope, with coin C beneath it, is then placed over coin A, care being taken not to let the two coins " chink " against each other or, as conjurers say, not to let the coins " talk." During all these movements you continue your story, saying: " It does not matter which two coins are visible so long as two are invisible, as we have them now."

These movements, which have taken so long to describe, take only a few moments to make, and they must be practised until they can be made with the utmost precision. When coin C is picked up beneath the envelope no movement of the fingers must be visible to the spectators and you must not look at your hands while you are doing this, nor pause in your speech. And the left hand must approach at exactly the right moment to cover the abstraction of the coin.

You now pick up coin D with the right hand while your left hand takes hold of the near left hand corner of the napkin and raises it a little from the table. The napkin is held between the first finger and thumb with the middle fingers left free. The right hand, holding coin D, goes beneath the napkin and, without the slightest pause or hesitation, deposits the coin upon the waiting left middle fingers and continues beneath the napkin until it is underneath the two coins at corner A. It gives a little flick to the napkin, making the coins clink against each other and displacing the envelope to show two. The effect is as though the coin had passed through the fabric of the napkin.

The right hand is immediately withdrawn from beneath the napkin and it picks up the displaced envelope. The left hand releases its hold of the corner of the napkin and, at the same moment, the right hand places the envelope into the left hand, thus covering the coin D. The envelope, with its concealed coin, is then replaced over the other two, care being taken, once more, not to let the coins talk.

There are now three coins under the envelope at A and one, uncovered, at B. The spectators believe there are only two at A and that one is under the second envelope at C. (You will notice that you are always one move ahead of your audience, a stratagem very common in magic and generally called the One-ahead Principle.)

The coin at corner B is now passed through the napkin in exactly the same way. The right hand lifts the envelope to show three coins at A and transfers it to the left hand to cover the fourth coin. The envelope, with the coin, is then replaced at A.

The last coin, you say, you will pass through the covering envelope instead of through the napkin. With your left hand you slightly raise the envelope at corner C and, placing your right hand beneath it, you pretend to remove the coin. Holding your hand exactly as you would if the coin were held between the fingers and thumb, you bring it over the envelope at A and about a foot above it. Your left hand you drop to your side, where you hold the other envelope between first finger and thumb. You press the tip of your left second finger firmly against the first finger nail. The right hand pretends to drop the coin it is supposed to hold and, at the same moment, the left second finger is allowed to slip off the first finger nail and strike the envelope with a resounding " whack." The effect is both surprising and amusing. Allow the spectators to see that the right hand is empty and then daintily lift the envelope to show the arrival of the fourth coin.

We have reached a point when, we think, we should talk to you about practising. Beginners are invariably too enthusiastic and try to show their new tricks to their friends before they have really learnt them. The result is generally disastrous, but it usually takes some time for the truth to be realized, that, however simple a conjuring trick may seem, it cannot be done successfully without a good deal of practice. Professional conjurers of long experience realize this full well and never dream of attempting to show a trick until they have run through it, privately, some dozens of times. Moderate your enthusiasm then, practise your tricks well, and you will be saved many moments of vexation.

The principle of Simulation which we have examined is the basis of a large number of methods by which small objects can be vanished. The books on conjuring are full of these methods, all slightly different from one another, but all based upon the same idea .... the simulation of the action of taking something in one hand, or of putting it into that hand, while the object is really retained, concealed, in the other hand. And this brings us to:

PALMING

When an object is thus concealed in the hand we say that it is " Palmed " although, originally, that meant holding it by a slight contraction of the palm of the hand. It is neither particularly easy nor particularly difficult to do, but it requires some practice. Place a coin (say a half-dollar) on the palm of the open hand, rather towards the wrist, and then very slightly contract the hand so as to grip the coin by its edges between the fleshy base of the thumb and the opposite edge of the palm. After some practice you will find that you can hold the coin quite securely and freely use all your fingers. Practice it at odd moments. Practice also, balancing the coin on the tips of the two middle fingers with the hand held in the position shown in Fig. 1, and bending the fingers inward to press the coin into the palm, where it can be securely held.

Practice palming other small objects also, a ball, a cork, a piece of sugar .... anything that is not very heavy. Try to hold the hand loosely and naturally, *as though it were*

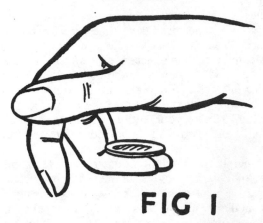

FIG I

empty, and learn to use the fingers freely. It is this last point, the freedom of the fingers, that makes true palming superior to Finger Palming and Thumb Palming, which we shall next describe, but for all that, many highly skilled performers have never used the true palm.

We will teach you the Finger Palm by showing you how you can use it to vanish a coin.

Toss a coin into the air, perhaps a foot, and let it fall, flat, upon the centre of the two middle fingers of the right hand. Bring the left hand up to the side of the right and turn the latter so that the coin falls from the fingers into the left hand. Immediately close the left hand upon the coin. Repeat this several times until the action is thoroughly familiar to you and then do it once more with the following slight difference. As you turn the right hand to tip the coin into the left, contract the right middle fingers so as to grip the coin by its sides, and retain it in the right hand. Close the left hand as though the coin had fallen into it, *exactly as you did before*, then move the left hand away and let the right, with the finger palmed coin, fall naturally to the side. *Keep your eyes on the left hand.* Pause a moment or two and then blow gently on the closed left fingers before opening them to show that the coin has disappeared.

Fig. 2 shows a coin held in the Finger-palm as you

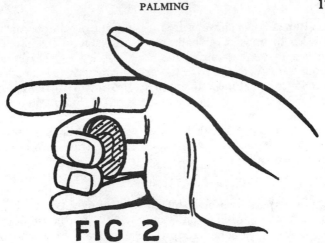

FIG 2

yourself see it. The hand, with its slightly pointing finger looks very natural and innocent to a spectator, and it is an excellent palm for many objects besides coins, and especially for comparatively heavy objects.

In another form of the Finger-palm, very useful for small balls and other round or roundish objects, the article is gripped by contracting the little finger alone, as shown in Fig. 3. In practice the ball, for instance, is held, first,

FIG 3

between the right first finger and thumb. The left hand is

held open and palm upwards. The right hand approaches the left to transfer the ball and, as the back of the hand is turned to the spectators, the ball is rolled by the thumb from the first to the little finger, and there held. The left hand is closed at the moment precisely necessary to complete the illusion. It is, again, a question of Simulation and Timing.

When you can satisfactorily execute this little manoeuvre you will be ready to attempt one more trick, a fine one which we call:

THE SURPRISING TUMBLER

You require a sheet of business letter paper, a tumbler, and a one dollar bill. The latter you will, in exercise of the conjurer's time honoured privilege, borrow from one of your spectators. You seat yourself at the table and, placing the tumbler mouth downward in front of you, wrap the paper round the tumbler to make a close fitting cover to ·it, and twist the top of the paper to keep it from unwrapping. You must mould the paper closely to the form of the tumbler and make sure that the glass is completely covered by the paper. Take the one dollar bill and crumple it into a ball, placing it by the side of the covered tumbler. Gaze rather critically at the two objects as though they were in the wrong positions and then move them, lifting the covered tumbler with the right hand by grasping it near the table, between the first finger and thumb, and replacing it upon a different part of the table. Now pick up the one dollar bill and apparently place it into the left hand, but really retain it in the right in the crook of the little finger. Lift the covered tumbler once more, as before, with the right first finger and thumb and, as you replace it, turn the hand slightly so that the palmed bill comes under the rim of the tumbler. Replace the tumbler in a slightly different position, leaving the bill beneath.

You now hold your left hand over the tumbler and tell the spectators you are going to make the bill pass from the hand into the tumbler. You make a little rubbing movement with your left fingers and slowly open them to show that the bill has gone.

With your right hand you lift the covered tumbler and reveal the bill.

As the attention of the spectators is drawn to the bill, the right hand carries the covered tumbler to the edge of the table, where the left hand meets it. The left fingers go inside the tumbler as the right hand slackens its grasp on the paper. The tumbler slides rapidly out of the paper cover and is held by the left fingers just underneath the edge of the table while the left thumb rests naturally on the table top. The right hand calmly replaces the cover alone above the rolled up bill. (In the last sentence the word *calmly* is the operative one. The slightest haste, the slightest flurry, will raise the suspicions of the spectators.) Because of the stiffness of the paper, and the moulding you gave it, it retains the shape of the glass and stands up unaltered.

You are ready now for a major miracle.

You announce your intention of making the bill disappear from under the tumbler. You hold your right hand over the cover and pause for a moment while you glance round the attentive audience. Then you suddenly slap your hand down upon the cover and crush it flat.

Reach well under the table with the left hand and tap the tumbler against the underside. As you do so, pick up the crumpled paper with the right hand and turn it over, and you will find that you can succeed in managing to slip the one dollar bill out of the paper and conceal it in your hand. Toss the crushed paper aside, and, as you bring the tumbler from under the table take it in your right hand and drop the bill inside it. You thus produce the illusion that both the tumbler *and the bill* were passed through the table.

Just as you should, *as a general rule*, never repeat a trick (and you should always remember this when you are asked, as you often will be, to " do it again ") so, *as a general thing*, you should not tell your audience exactly what you are about to do. Forewarned they will be better armed against your wiles and your trick will become much more difficult to execute successfully. Notice that in the foregoing trick you tell the audience that you are going to make the bill pass from the hand into the tumbler only *after it is already there*, unknown to them.

We now come to a very famous trick which has been performed in various ways by many famous magicians. It was one of the favourite pocket tricks of the celebrated Houdini. It employs a principle we have not previously introduced you to, that of *Duplication*. It is called:

THE THREE PELLETS

You begin by tearing a corner from a newspaper (the size of this piece you will find from experience) and, from it, you make three tightly rolled paper pellets each about the size of a large pea. Unknown to your spectators you have concealed in your left hand a *duplicate*, a fourth pellet which you have previously made. You hold the pellet concealed in your hand by bending the second, third, and fourth fingers quite naturally, leaving the first finger free to be used, with the thumb, in making the visible pellets which you throw upon the table. You also have, in your right coat pocket, a larger pellet or ball of newspaper, or, if you prefer, a golf ball, a small tomato, or any object of convenient size to conceal in the hand.

You begin by showing your right hand empty. With the left hand you pick up two of the pellets and drop them into the right, dropping the concealed pellet with them and immediately closing the hand. You pick up the third pellet with the left hand and pretend to drop it into your pocket, but really you keep it in the hand, concealed by clipping it between the tips of the first and second fingers. You utter the magic word " Abracadabra " and, opening the right hand, let the THREE pellets fall on to the table.

With the left hand you gather the three pellets together and pick them up, holding them all at the tips of the fingers. The fourth pellet will be hidden behind them and the hand appears to hold only three. You show the right hand empty and drop all the pellets into it. Then, with the left hand obviously empty, you remove one pellet from the right, which you pretend to place in your pocket as before. Again you pronounce the magic word and open the right hand to show three pellets once more.

Now the left hand apparently picks up the three pellets from the open right hand and drops them on the table. Really only two pellets are taken and the third is the one that was concealed at the left finger tips. One pellet is left in the right hand, which is immediately turned so that the pellet is concealed. The right hand then picks up a pellet and drops it into the left. Next it does the same with the second pellet, this time dropping the concealed one also. The right hand then takes the third pellet, *really* drops it into the pocket, and fingerpalms the tomato, golf ball, or whatever article you use. Again the magic word is pronounced and the left hand opened to show three pellets once more.

All the preceding actions have been briskly performed, but now you go still faster. The right hand gathers up two of the pellets and pretends to place them into the left. Actually the tomato is dropped into the left hand, which at once closes upon it, and the pellets are simply retained behind the tips of the right fingers. These fingers immediately pick up the third pellet and all three are at once dropped into the right coat pocket.

Once more you pronounce the magic word "Abracadabra" and ask the spectators what you have in your left hand. "Three pellets," they say and, with a look of feigned astonishment, you open your hand to show the tomato, saying, "What makes you think that?"

We have described the last trick as performed with pellets of paper but it can be performed with all kinds of small objects. Some performers are fond of doing it at the table with pellets of bread, others use pieces of match stick, and it can also be done with lumps of sugar. It is also capable of a great deal of variation, as you will discover for yourself when you grow more expert. It is not too early

to impress upon you the need to think for yourself if you
desire to succeed in conjuring. Having first learnt to
perform a trick as we describe it, see if you can introduce
some *personal* variation into it to alter it, however slightly.
It is too early to expect you to evolve original tricks for
yourself but it is not too soon for you to try to introduce
some slight variations.

We think it is time to speak to you now about

PATTER

the words a conjurer uses when he is performing, which are
not always so unconsidered as they may seem. There is a
fashion at the moment, a fashion which we think is on the
wane, for conjurers to be also comedians or, at least, for
conjurers to attempt to be also comedians, for many of
them are very sad comics. To understand this tendency we
must consider a little of the history of conjuring.

A century ago people would flock to see anything that
was marvellous, anything that they could not understand.
The few conjurers of the time, in spite of the profound
limitations of their technique, had no difficulty in holding
the attention of their audiences, to whom their tricks were
astonishing and inexplicable mysteries, and they presented
their feats seriously. Then came the twentieth century,
with its scientific revolution, to produce a public surrounded
always by inexplicable mysteries and satiated with marvels.
The petty mysteries of the conjurer became rather insigni-
ficant face to face with the marvels of modern science.
Conjurers began to bolster up their tricks, first with humour
and later with comedy, and gradually the fashion of the
chattering, humorous, conjurer was developed.

But of recent years there has been a drift in the opposite
direction. Conjurers have again discovered that conjuring
presented as conjuring is just as entertaining, and can be
just as amusing, as when it is presented with comedy—and
that it can also be mystifying, while the element of mystery
is killed when comedy is added.

We mention all this to reassure you. It is not necessary

to be a comedian to become a conjurer. On the other hand there is no need to be grim and solemn. Be yourself, but be yourself at your best, let us even suggest that you be yourself a little improved, particularly in your speech.

When you set out to do a conjuring trick you must know precisely what you are going to do and there is no reason why you should not also know what you will say. We do not suggest that you should learn every word by heart, as earlier writers have insisted and many conjurers do, but we do suggest that you should know your " main headings," as public speakers do, that is to say, know the general drift of your talk. You will never then be entirely at a loss for words and you will find that, when you have done a trick a few dozen times, you will say much the same things every time you do it. You will then have " set patter " for your trick which will have *grown* to fit you and which you will be able to use with success.

Do not be afraid to put a joke or two into your patter, *if the jokes fit*, but do not drag in jokes simply for the sake of something to say, or to make a trick last longer. Above all, do not make a joke at the climax of a trick, when the spectators should be agreeably surprised by the unexpected ending which all good tricks have, and you do not want to spoil their appreciation with the distraction of a joke.

Finally, avoid the obvious and do not be afraid to keep silent when you have nothing interesting to say.

Let us now go back to our first trick, the Coin through the Hand, and give another version of it which will also provide a further example of the use of duplicates. For facility of reference we will call this version

THE BEWILDERING COIN

You will require two half-dollars (or quarters) as nearly alike as possible. One of these you drop into your left sleeve, where it will rest quite safely against your fore-arm as long as you keep your arm bent. When you drop your arm to your side the coin will fall into the left hand and be caught by the half closed fingers. Try this once or twice first.

Crumple a $5 bill into a ball and place it in your right trouser pocket.

Now, with the duplicate coin in your left sleeve, you perform your trick of the coin passing through the hand. At its conclusion you open your left hand to show the coin lying on its palm. You pick up this coin with the right hand and let the left hand drop to the side. The duplicate coin slides into the left hand and you are ready to repeat the trick.

Bring the slightly closed left hand up in front of you, breast high, and tap the coin on the back of the hand. Let the coin slide behind the middle fingers as before. Now raise the right hand a few inches, bend the middle fingers, with the coin balanced on them as shown in Figure 1, carry the coin smartly into the palm, and bring the fingers down flat upon the back of the left hand. Make a little rubbing movement and then raise the fingers to show that the coin has passed through the hand again (!) and open the left hand to show it there.

The visible coin is now lying flat upon the palm of the left hand. The second coin is palmed in the right hand. The right hand picks up the visible coin by its edges, between the first and second fingers. This brings the right palm immediately above the left middle fingers and, as the visible coin is picked up, the palmed one is dropped into the left hand, which slightly closes and turns a little to conceal the coin. The right hand then, apparently, drops its coin into the right trouser pocket, but, as soon as the hand is within the pocket, the middle fingers press the coin into the palm and the hand is withdrawn with the coin concealed.

You now blow gently upon the back of your left hand, which you turn over and slowly open to show another half-dollar. With a smile of pleasure you pick the coin up, exactly as before, allowing the palmed coin to fall into the left hand, which turns and closes enough to hide it. This time you really drop the coin into your pocket and palm in its stead the rolled up $5 bill.

Again you blow upon your left hand and open it to show

another coin. You pick up the coin and drop the $5 bill into the hand in its place. With a satisfied smile you drop the half-dollar into your pocket, and, once more, you blow gently upon the back of your left hand.

Your look of satisfaction changes to one of consternation. You open your hand and reveal the crumpled bill. You open the bill with a frown and say: "I'm sorry . . . something went wrong!"

Notice the use of the coat sleeve in the last example for, in spite of the popularity of the explanation " up his sleeve," the sleeves are not often used in modern conjuring. There is, however, an excellent little impromptu trick which makes very good use of the coat sleeve, which we will call

THE FLYING DIME

You hold a Liberty head dime by its edge between the tips of the first finger and thumb, and call attention to the winged head that appears on one side. You cover the dime with the fingers of the other hand for a moment, and order the winged head to fly away. The coin disappears and is found behind a spectator's ear, or in a similarly amusing place.

To perform the trick, hold the dime at the tips of the first finger and thumb, supported by the second finger as shown in Fig. 4. Now bring the right hand, held

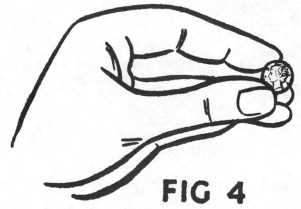

FIG 4

perfectly flat, above the coin, and cover it with the fingers for a moment. The right hand and forearm must be held in one straight line and brought above the coin in such a way that the left fingers point straight up the right sleeve. As soon as the dime is covered, squeeze it firmly between the finger and thumb so that it shoots straight up the right sleeve. It is propelled in precisely the same way that children squirt orange pips between finger and thumb. Remove the right hand to show that the coin has disappeared.

Reach out with the empty left hand and pretend to find the coin behind someone's ear. At the same moment drop the right hand to the side and permit the coin to fall out of the sleeve into the hand. Then slap the left fingers down upon the right as though placing the coin upon the right fingers, and move the left hand away, leaving the coin lying upon the right. The illusion is perfect if the timing is good.

If you have been practising your palming you should now be sufficiently advanced to tackle a very famous trick which we will call

THE COIN AND THE HAT

A coin disappears several times and is found each time under a hat and, finally and unexpectedly, a large and surprising object is found under the hat. Many performers produce as the final surprise a pint glass full of beer or water, others find a guinea pig under the hat. The famous Max Malini, who wandered about the world for years, performing for the most part at private clubs, would often finish this trick by producing a large and heavy stone or a piece of a brick, and is supposed to have had a special pocket made in his clothes to enable him to carry the weighty object without discomfort. We suggest that you use a large potato, a grapefruit, or something similar. Put this in your left hand coat pocket. Borrow a hat, preferably a deby, and a half-dollar.

Spin the coin into the air and catch it on the fingers of the right hand. Pretend to drop it into the left hand but really finger-palm it in the right (as previously described) and close the left hand as if it held the coin. Pick up the hat with the right hand, the fingers going inside it and holding the coin against the lining. Hold the hat at arms length and, with a little tossing movement towards the hat, open the left hand and show that the coin has vanished. A split second afterwards let the coin drop from the right fingers, to fall, audibly, into the hat.

Transfer the hat to the left hand, holding it in the same way again, fingers inside, and remove the coin from the hat with the right hand. Hold the hat at arms length again, and pretend to throw the coin high into the air. Actually, as the hand swings down the coin is pressed into the palm by the two middle fingers and then the hand swings up in the motion of throwing, with the fingers slightly apart. You follow the supposed flight of the coin with your eyes and follow it also as it seems to fall into the hat with an audible thud. This sound you produce by pressing your second finger tip against your first finger nail, inside the hat, and then letting it slip off to strike the side of the hat with a resounding " wallop " at the proper moment. Some people may find it easier to do this by pressing the *third* finger upon the *second* finger nail. Hands differ in their formation and it does not matter at all how these little things are done so long as the desired effect is produced. Always remember this when reading books on conjuring which try to maintain that there is a right and a wrong way to do these little sleights.

Now, with your right hand, you reach into the hat and remove the coin, showing it to the spectators.

Next you repeat the whole of the last phase. You apparently throw the coin into the air, really palming it in the right hand, and you pretend to catch it in the hat, where it is again heard to fall. You reach into the hat and, without making any sound, you leave the palmed coin in the bottom of the hat and bring out the hand as though it held the coin. You immediately put the hat down on the table, and then you pretend to put the coin into your left hand. After a moments pause you make a throwing movement towards the hat and open the left hand to show it empty.

With the right hand you lift the hat and turn it over, allowing the coin to fall on to the table. At the same moment your left hand takes the potato from your pocket and, as all eyes turn to the falling coin, the right hand puts the hat into the left, *over the potato.* The coin is picked up and the hat put down with the potato underneath it.

Once more the coin is apparently dropped into the left hand while it is really finger-palmed in the right. Another pass is made towards the hat and the coin shown to have disappeared. The hat is lifted to show the potato, the appearance of which comes as a complete and rather comical surprise.

We shall now give you a trick of an entirely different kind, of great interest because it is capable of so many variations. It is called

THE KNIFE AND THE PAPERS

Tear, or cut, six small pieces of paper, a little less than half an inch square (pieces cut from the margin of a newspaper will do well), damp them with water, and stick them to the blade of a table knife, three on each side, about an inch apart from each other. Hold the knife with the blade pointing slightly downward, thumb on top and fingers beneath the handle, as shown in Fig. 5, which shows your own view of the hand and knife.

With your right thumb slide the first piece of paper (the one nearest the handle) off the knife, crumple it slightly, and pretend to throw it away, but actually retain it in the hand, clipped between the tips of the first and second fingers. Now appear to show the other side of the knife by turning the hand over towards you to reach the position shown in Fig. 6, but, as the hand turns over, revolve the knife also, by pushing slightly with the left thumb and pulling a little with the first finger, so that the same side of the blade is again shown to the spectators. Simultaneously

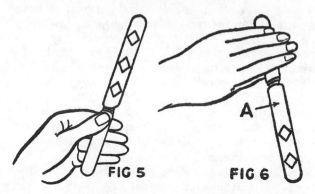

FIG 5   FIG 6

the right first and second finger tips cover the portion of
the knife from which the paper has been removed (the
portion marked A in Fig. 6) and pretend to remove a
second piece of paper. Actually they show the first piece
which they had concealed and which is now really thrown
away.

The hand is now turned back to the first position (that
of Fig. 5) and once more the knife is twisted between
the fingers, this time in the opposite direction, and the knife
appears to have been shown on both sides. The little twist
of the knife is completely hidden by the larger turn of the
whole hand, and the illusion is perfect.

The knife is once more shown on both sides, the little
twist being made in order to show the same side each time,
and the knife appears to have only two pieces of paper on
each side. With a wave of the arm the knife is quickly
turned between the fingers and one paper is seen to have
returned to the blade.

Another wave of the knife and the second paper appears
to have returned to it, the knife being shown, by means of
the twist, apparently to have three papers on both sides
again.

You now pretend to remove all six papers, although you
actually remove only the two that remain on one side of the
knife, leaving the other three undisturbed. To do this

first wave the knife from side to side, turn it between the fingers, and clap the right middle fingers against the point A of Fig. 6 and pretend to remove the paper that is supposed to be at that point. Quickly turn the hand over (giving the knife a twist again) and pretend to remove the paper from the opposite side. Next, actually remove the centre paper from the side of the knife now facing the spectators, then turn the hand and *pretend* to remove the piece from the opposite side. You can now, by means of the twist, apparently show the knife to have only one piece of paper on each side.

Repeat the previous moves apparently to remove the last piece of paper from each side but only remove one piece. Then, with the twist, show the knife on both sides.

Command three of the papers to return. Wave the knife, give it a twist, and show the papers to be back.

Command the other three papers to return, and by means of the twist, show three papers on both sides of the knife.

Then wipe the papers from the knife and drop them into your pocket. Put the knife down for curious persons to inspect it . . . . .

The description has involved us in a good deal of unvoidable repetition and we hope you have followed us with knife and papers in your hands. We have described the trick as done with the knife held in the left hand, but if you find it easier to hold it with the right hand, by all means do so. All sorts of variations can be introduced into the trick and it can also take different forms, such as the little bat with three holes, and a peg which jumps from hole to hole, the bat that is marked with a piece of chalk, and various " paddle " tricks, specially made, which are sold by the dealers in conjuring apparatus.

There are many excellent little tricks which, while hardly important enough to stand alone, create considerable amusement when performed impromptu or when introduced in between more impressive mysteries. Amongst those which you should add to your repertoire is

THE JUMPING RUBBER BAND

Place a small rubber band around the roots of the left first and second fingers. Hold the left hand palm upwards and catch hold of the band with the right first finger and thumb. Stretch it towards yourself and let it fly back again. Stretch it towards yourself again and close the left fingers into a fist, so that all the fingers go inside the band. Release the band and quickly turn the hand over so that the fact that the fingers are within the band is not observed. Press the tip of the thumb against the band where it passes round the first finger, the point marked "A" in Fig. 7,

FIG 7   FIG 8

so as to stretch the band a little, and release it with a slight flick. The band will fly from the first and second fingers to encircle the third and fourth.

Open the fingers to display the hand from both sides with the rubber band around the third and fourth fingers. With the hand held palm downwards, insert the tip of the left thumb into the band and raise it from the fingers. Then close the hand into a fist, letting the tips of the fingers go inside the band again. Now remove the thumb. Open the fingers very slightly, to stretch the band, and it will fly back to its first position on the first and second fingers.

To finish the trick, put one end of the band over the tip of the first finger, carry the band behind the second finger, and then slip the other end over the first finger-tip again, as shown in Fig. 8. Be careful not to twist the band. Ask someone to hold the tip of your first finger in order " to keep the band from escaping." When the finger is firmly held, quickly slip the second finger out of the band. The band will fly across the room, and sometimes disappear completely.

With a little more difficulty the first part of the trick may be done with two rubber bands of different colours, one around the first two and the other around the last two fingers. At your command the bands change places. It is only necessary to stretch both bands at once and insert the tips of the fingers as you close the hand.

There are also many excellent little tricks with matches and match boxes, of which we will mention

THE ANIMATED MATCH-BOX

This is most mysterious if it is well done. Take your match-box and open it about an eighth of an inch to ascertain which way the drawer is facing. Now place the box on the back of the left hand, the bottom of the drawer uppermost, so that the end of the open drawer comes over the knuckle of the second finger, and close the box so as to catch between the drawer and the box a little of the loose flesh that lies above the knuckle of the middle finger. Keep the hand perfectly flat while doing this. Make one or two " passes " over the box, as if to " hypnotize " it, and then very slightly bend the middle fingers downward. The flesh over the knuckles being straightened by this action the box will be pulled up and will stand on its end. When you straighten the fingers, again, in response, of course, to "hypnotic passes," the match box will lie down again. With a little practice you will find yourself able to make the box rise and fall twice before the little piece of loose flesh works its way out of the box. Then the box is tossed into the air and you proceed with your mysteries.

When you have lit your cigarette you can try

DOWN YOUR SLEEVE

You hold the lighted match at arm's length in your right hand. You blow strongly down your *left* sleeve . . . . and extinguish the match! Impossible? Of course.

Hold the lighted match between the first and second finger tips in the same way that you hold a cigarette which you have taken from your lips, horizontally, clipped between the fingers. As you blow down your left sleeve, and the spectators watch you do so, you put the tip of your thumb against the end of the match, behind the fingers, press down firmly on the match, and then, suddenly, release it. The resulting " Flick " sends a sudden shock through the match, which extinguishes the flame.

The same principle is responsible for the amusing

MAGNETIC MATCH

Take two matches from the box and place the latter on the table. Lay one match upon the box so that the head end overhangs the edge. Rub the head of the other match briskly on your sleeve to " magnetize" it. Now slowly bring the head of the match you hold beneath the head of the other match and, as soon as the two heads touch, the match lying on the box flies up into the air.

Hold your match in the normal manner between the first finger and thumb. Hold it firmly and, underneath the thumb, press the tip of your second finger against the end of the match. As the two match heads touch, let the tip of the second finger slip off the match. The shock, running through the match, passes into the second one and flings it into the air in an astonishing way.

We think you will have learnt much from the study of these impromptu tricks. You will have learnt that conjuring is not a simple matter of the quickness of the hand but that it is a kind of *acting* that uses as its chief weapons imitation and simulation and the ability to do two things at the same moment, the thing the spectators see and the thing they do not see. You will have learnt also that all these things depend upon proper *timing*. If, in addition, you have gained some little experience of actual conjuring, you will now be able to tackle some more studied mysteries.

PART II

STUDIED MYSTERIES

In this, the larger part of our Handbook, we shall give you a repertoire of conjuring tricks for set performances, tricks requiring, at times, a little preparation and a few small properties, but never tricks requiring bulky or expensive apparatus. Your first performances will be given in your own home, or the homes of friends, before a limited number of people and you will neither require nor have any use for tricks with much apparatus.

In arranging a set programme one of the most important points to consider is the proper routining of the material available. It is not sufficient to do six tricks one after the other and call that a " show." They must be arranged in the best order. Generally one should end the show with one's best effect and one should start with a fairly short and surprising trick. The object of this is to get the full attention of the audience as quickly as possible. The tricks that come in between should be arranged to give as much variety as possible.

But other things must also be taken into consideration. There are technical points to think about. For instance, one trick may require that you drop a coin, unseen and unheard, into your left coat pocket. Another trick may require that you have a tumbler in that pocket. Obviously you must do the trick with the tumbler first, to empty the pocket, but the Author will confess that he once, in his youthful days, vanished a borrowed watch and dropped it into a tumbler that was in his pocket! The nerve shattering crash of the watch in the tumbler reverberates through his dreams to this day.

But it is another kind of routining we will mention here, that of linking two or three small effects together to make one more or less imposing *routine*. And, if we may digress for a moment, we would here discuss the use of the words *trick* and *effect*. We have used the word *trick* in this Handbook in its popular sense, as it is used in the phrase, " a conjuring trick." But, led by the 19th century author of conjuring books, Professor Hoffmann, and supported by most subsequent writers, conjurers generally prefer not to use this word, which they consider beneath the dignity of their Art in this application. They prefer to use the word *trick* to designate the method or device the conjurer uses, and to speak of the result of the use of that method or device (or of a combination of various methods and devices) as an *effect*, a *problem*, or an *experiment*. Personally we have no passion for lost causes and shall continue to talk, as everyone does, of *conjuring tricks, EXCEPT WHEN WE ARE PERFORMING THEM*, when we shall shun the word " trick " like poison, just as we shall shun anything else which would remind our audience that there may be anything spurious about the mysteries we show them. When you present a conjuring performance you must try to lead your audience to join you in creating a world of make-believe in which the impossible can, and does happen. You will no more mention tricks than you will show them the false bottom of the magic canister or the coin concealed in the left palm. These are the skeletons in the cupboard that must always be closed.

And now we will return to our routining of small tricks with an example we will call

A PROBLEM IN SUSPENSION

First you must make for yourself a simple piece of apparatus with a length of fine cat-gut, such as anglers use for casts, a good elastic band or short piece of cord elastic, and a safety pin. Form the cat-gut (which should be about nine inches long) into a loop and tie it to the elastic band. Pin the other end of the elastic to the inside of your right coat sleeve. You must adjust the pin so that the loop of gut will lie just inside the coat sleeve. Next provide yourself with a small beer bottle of very dark opaque glass, a piece of stout picture cord about a yard long, a table knife, and a little cork ball small enough to slip easily through the mouth of the bottle. This ball you can cut from an ordinary cork and round with sand paper. It should then be blackened with ink.

Fold the cord into four and push it half way into the bottle, then place the little cork ball in the mouth of the bottle so that it is hidden by the cord, which also keeps it from falling inside. Presently, when you take the cord out of the bottle, you will be able to secretly obtain possession of the ball. Put the bottle and the knife on your table and, with the cat-gut loop in your sleeve, you are ready to perform.

You can very well use this routine as your " opening " or commencing effect, in which case, before you come forward, you draw the loop out of your sleeve and slip it over the tip of the second finger, allowing the gut to go under the finger nail. The loop will lie close beneath the hand and when the back of the hand is turned upwards only a little piece of gut on either side of the nail will be visible.

If you do not use this trick as your opening one the best time to put the loop into position is *at the conclusion of the preceding trick*. You can pull the loop down quite deliberately and slip it on your finger tip as you bow to acknowledge the applause that greeted the termination of your trick, or you can do it as you turn to replace something on your table.

But the important thing is that you should plan your procedure beforehand and *rehearse it*. No part of a conjuring trick should be left to chance and you should go over every part of it, in private, many times, before you attempt to do it in public, even before the limited public of your personal friends.

So, with the loop in position on your second finger, which must from now on be kept quite straight, or the loop will slip off and be drawn up the right sleeve by the elastic, you commence the trick by picking up the knife, which you hold in your left hand. You briskly rub the blade of the knife with the right fingers, as if to magnetise it, and allow the knife to pass between the loop of gut and the four fingers. Then you spread the fingers wide apart, pressing downwards with the first and fourth, and leave the knife, apparently clinging to the fingers, but really supported by the tension of the elastic. Fig. 9 shows an underneath

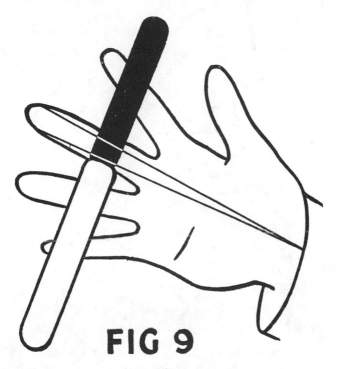

FIG 9

view of this, a view which must never be seen by the spectators. The hand is displayed in various positions, always with its back to the spectators, the knife clinging fast to the fingers.

The left hand then grasps the knife by the handle, the

right second finger bends slightly to release the loop of gut, and the loop flies invisibly up the sleeve.

The right fingers return to the knife blade, the second, third and fourth fingers being placed against the side of the blade while the first finger *tip* is placed against the *edge* of the knife, as shown in Fig. 10. The knife again clings

FIG 10

to the fingers, the weight of the handle keeping the knife point firmly against the first finger tip. The hand can be displayed in all positions and it is even possible to remove the third and fourth fingers from the blade. Finally, a spectator may be allowed to remove the knife from the finger-tips.

You now pick up the bottle, remove the cord, conceal

the little ball in your hand, and pass the bottle and cord
for inspection, apologizing perhaps for the absence of the
beer. While the articles are being inspected you " thumb-
palm " the ball, that is to say, you roll it with the first and
second fingers into the fork of the thumb and grip it there
against the side of the hand as shown in Fig. 11. You

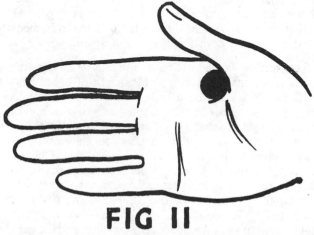

FIG II

now retrieve your properties, the cord with the left hand,
the bottle with the right. You grasp the bottle by its neck
between fingers and thumb and let it swing between the
fingers so that its mouth comes just beneath the thumb-
palmed ball. You at once release the ball so that it falls
into the bottle.

Very slowly and deliberately you lower one end of the
cord into the bottle. When half the cord is in the bottle
you turn it upside down and let go of the cord. The cork
ball runs into the neck of the bottle and wedges the cord,
which hangs there, " supported entirely by voluntary con-
tributions," as David Devant*used to say in a similar case.

Let the cord swing for a little while and then grasp it in
the left hand and reverse the position of the things, allowing
the bottle to swing gently on the cord. The little ball

*An illustrious magician of our times.

wedges firmly in the neck of the bottle and holds it quite securely.

Now, with the right hand held palm upwards, grasp the bottle by its neck, close to the mouth, between the first and second fingers and thumb, and pull the cord out of the bottle. Pull firmly and steadily, without displaying any effort, and the ball will roll out with the cord, into the bend of the third and fourth fingers, and can be " palmed " in similar manner to that illustrated by Fig. 3. Immediately hand bottle and cord for inspection again.

The routine is of particular interest as illustrating the combination of apparatus and sleight-of-hand, and the repetition of a trick by a different method. The effect of the first levitation of the knife by means of the elastic is enhanced by the second levitation by the hand alone.

The practice of handing articles to the spectators for examination or inspection is not generally to be recommended. Interesting though it may be perhaps, to the persons invited to inspect the apparatus, it is not very entertaining to the rest of the company, and unduly drags out a trick. It should only be done when it is thought that examination of the properties may increase the effectiveness of the trick. In the present case, unless the articles are handed for inspection, the audience will probably conclude that the knife is coated with some sticky substance and that the bottle is fitted with some kind of hook. Incidentally, try, when you can, to hear the theories and opinions of your friends as to how your effects are produced. They will always be interesting and sometimes they will be instructive.

We shall now turn to a new theme, that of destruction and restoration, an effect which conjurers produce in many different forms. We will take, first, a simple sleight-of-hand version, which may be done with

PAPER NAPKINS

You require two paper napkins, one of which you privately

squeeze into a ball and conceal in the bend of the left elbow. Simply place the ball of paper on the inside of your arm, at the joint, and bend the arm so that the ball disappears within the folds of the coat, where it will remain concealed as long as you keep the arm bent. You can easily put the balled napkin in position as you turn to your table to pick up the other one, which should be there ready, neatly folded in four.

The napkin, by the way, should not be simply rolled up. First crush the paper in one direction to make a rough " wick " and then crush it the other way into a rough ball. Later, when you desire to open it, you can do so in two movements, first pulling the ball into a " wick " again and then opening that sideways. It is taking care of little points like this that makes the difference between the good conjurer, who is attractive and elegant in all he does, and the uninstructed amateur who fumbles everything he touches.

Open the folded napkin and display it, deliberately, on both sides, holding it throughout between the first fingers and thumbs, with the palms of the hands towards the audience. We have seen so many bad conjurers spoil this, and other paper tearing tricks, by working with the backs of the hands to the spectators that we cannot too strongly emphasise this point—*palms always open to the audience please*.

Very deliberately tear the napkin into four pieces. Stand with the right side slightly turned away from the audience and hold the four pieces at the tips of the fingers of the right hand. With the left hand pull the right sleeve back a little by grasping the coat at the bend of the elbow and giving a little tug. Take the pieces of napkin in the left hand and proceed to pull back the left sleeve in just the same way, an action which quite naturally permits you to finger-palm the napkin from the bend of the elbow. Immediately place the four pieces in the left hand so that the finger-palmed ball of paper is concealed beneath them.

Now, using the right hand alone, slowly crumple the

pieces into a ball on top of the other ball concealed in the hand. Squeeze the two balls together and display them between the tips of the right finger and thumb. They appear as only one ball of paper. Turn them over so as to bring the duplicate napkin uppermost and then take the duplicate with the left hand, leaving the ball of pieces finger-palmed in the right. Blow gently upon the bundle held at the tips of the fingers of the left hand and, as you thus draw all attention to that hand, once more hitch the left sleeve back a little and leave the bundle of pieces in the bend of the elbow.

Daintily and deliberately undo the bundle and reveal the restored napkin.

Presently you must rid yourself of the bundle of pieces reposing in your sleeve. There is no hurry to do this and you tmust choose your opportunity to do it when the attention of the spectators is diverted to some other direction, perhaps at some time during the course of your next trick.

Make a mental note of this method of concealing a small object in the bend of the elbow. It can be used in other ways, particularly in opening tricks, when one can commence with the object already in place.

We will now discuss another version of the same effect which uses a different principle. We will call it

A STUDY IN BLACK AND WHITE

You will require some black and some white tissue paper. You will find that tissue paper bought by the quire will cut without waste into sheets about 15 inches by 10 inches. For each presentation of the trick you will require two pieces of black and two pieces of white. Put one of the black sheets on the table before you, so that its long edges are horizontal, and put a spot of paste about three inches in from its upper left hand corner. Take the second sheet of black and superimpose it exactly upon the first and press it down upon the paste. (It is desirable, of course, to prepare a number of sheets at the same time.) When the paste is dry, place one of the white sheets on the upper black one and roughly pleat them both together into a long strip about two inches wide. Then pleat the strip into a two inch square above the spot of paste and finally squeeze it into a rough ball. You now have a sheet of black tissue paper on the back of which reposes a bundle consisting of a piece of black and a piece of white. Put the other piece of white in front of the black, fold both together, and place them in your pocket, and you are ready to perform.

Unfold the black and white papers, taking care to keep the little bundle concealed behind them, and announce " a problem with the national colours of Scotland." Hold the papers by their corners with the fingers concealing the little bundle and you may show both sides.

Slowly and deliberately tear up the papers. Using only one hand, crumple the papers into a bundle and press this bundle against the concealed one. Display the papers deliberately at the finger tips, the two bundles pressed together and appearing as one, and then simply turn them over to bring the torn pieces to the rear. Slowly open the bundle of duplicate sheets to show the restored papers. The torn pieces remain concealed and attached to the black sheet.

Although the trick is very easy to do it requires a good deal of practice to do it really neatly and well, in fact we will here venture a general observation that the easiest tricks to do are often those that need the most practice to do really well.

The trick is of some interest because of the many variations of it that are possible. For instance, it is possible to tear up two sheets of black and white tissue and restore them as one sheet of black and white squares, representing a chess board. One can even produce simple designs, names, and messages.

Using the same principle (which is the principle of double facing) in a slightly different way, and joining another trick to it, we have an effect we will call

THE COUNTING CHALK

The total of the figures given by two dice shaken together in a tumbler appears, written in chalk, on a piece of black paper. That is the effect which the audience will remember.

Take two pieces of black tissue paper and attach them to each other with a spot of paste as you did for the preceding trick. Take two small pieces of white chalk, little more than half an inch long, chalk the figure 14 boldly on one of the pieces of paper, and crumple the paper into a ball with one of the pieces of chalk inside. Place the other piece of chalk on your table with two dice and a tumbler.

Commence the trick by dropping the dice into the tumbler and handing it to someone to hold. Then show the sheet of black tissue paper, keeping the rolled up duplicate concealed, crush it into a ball, and place it in some prominent position in the room.

Turn your back to the person holding the tumbler, so that you cannot see the dice, and instruct him to shake the dice thoroughly in the tumbler. When he is satisfied, tell him to look into the tumbler and add together the points shown by the two dice. When he has done that, tell him to hold the tumbler above his head, to look through the bottom of it, and to add to his previous figure the total of the points he then sees.

Take the piece of chalk and hold it for a moment against the man's forehead, asking him to think intently of the total which he has reached.

Pretend to put the chalk into your left hand, but really finger-palm it in your right. With a little tossing movement towards the black paper, open the left hand to show that the chalk has disappeared. Step over to the black paper and take the opportunity to drop the chalk into your pocket.

Hold the ball of paper up on high and ask the man to state the total given by the dice. It will always be fourteen, as we will presently explain. Deliberately open the paper ball. Out drops the missing (?) chalk, and on the paper is the figure 14!

It remains for us to explain why the total is always fourteen. Very few people besides conjurers and dice players (and dice players are not common in many areas) appear to be aware that the opposite sides of all properly made dice always total *seven*. That being so, as you can easily verify by inspection, the opposite sides of a pair of dice must always total fourteen. The use of the tumbler, as described, ensures that the opposite sides are, in fact, totalled, without calling attention to the fact.

Take care in this trick, to hand the tumbler and dice to a man who can count accurately beyond ten, a piece of advice which is not so futile as it may seem.

The last trick, while it used the same principle of Double Facing, departed from the theme of destruction and restoration, but we will return to that theme now. In the days of our grandfathers the most famous effect of this kind was the often done watch trick. The borrowed watch was smashed into pieces, loaded into a pistol, and fired at an ornamental target upon which it reappeared, restored to its former state. The trick has disappeared with the passing of the demand for conjuring with apparatus and with the introduction of wrist watches, whose flapping straps complicate the working of the trick. It is high time that, in spite of various difficulties, it was revived in modern form but, meanwhile, we will describe the trick that has replaced it, the burnt and restored Dollar Bill trick, which has many variations, of which we shall give you two examples, the first being

THE BILL AND THE CIGARETTE

You will require the following " properties ": a candle in a candlestick, an envelope, a box of matches, a pencil and a small white card (such as a visiting card), a cigarette, an ash tray, and a one-dollar bill.

First take the envelope and, with a sharp knife, cut a slit in its face, about an inch and a half long, in such a position that the slit cannot be seen from the back when the envelope s opened. Write with a pencil, in small figures, underneath

the flap at the right hand end, the number of your one
dollar bill, such as E 08326409 F.   This is illustrated by
Fig. 12 which also shows a folded Dollar Bill which

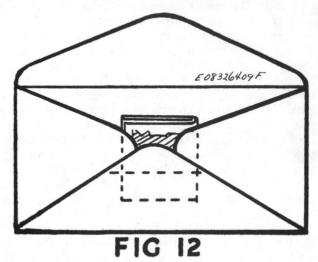

E08326409F.

FIG 12

has been pushed half way through the slit in the face of
the envelope, which is indicated by the dotted line.

Take the cigarette and remove some of the tobacco. Fold
the one dollar bill, roll it up tightly, and push it into the
cigarette. Replace a little of the tobacco above the note
and the cigarette will appear to be quite ordinary. Put
this cigarette in your right hand coat pocket with the box
of matches. The cigarette should lie in the pocket on the
outside of the box of matches.

With the pencil and visiting card in convenient pockets,
the ash tray and the envelope on your table with the candle
in its stick, you are ready to perform.

If you are performing to a fairly large audience it will be
sufficient to ask for the loan of a one dollar bill: you
are certain to have several offered to you and you can choose
one that resembles your own bill. Before a small company
it is a good scheme to make " a vote of confidence " of the

matter, and declare that you wish to know how many present would be prepared to lend you a one dollar bill. Several people will then offer you one and you can take the one that is most like your own for " wear and tear."

Remark that, while you are begging, you would like to ask for a cigarette also. When one is offered you, take it with your right hand. Hold the borrowed bill in your left hand and, having thanked the donor of the cigarette, thrust your right hand, cigarette and all, into your coat pocket and bring out the box of matches. You will remember we told you to put your prepared cigarette on the outside of the box of matches. As soon as your hand is inside the pocket you drop the borrowed cigarette on the left or inside of the box and then pick up the box and the prepared cigarette together and bring them out of the pocket. The action is made so natural by the presence of the Dollar Bill in the left hand that it passes without suspicion. Place the box in the left hand, with the bill, and put the cigarette between your lips. Then strike a match to light the cigarette but, as you go to do so, change your mind and light the candle instead. Drop the matches on the table.

Fold the borrowed bill three times, into halves, quarters, and then eighths. Pick up the envelope and half place the bill inside it, then, as an afterthought, withdraw the bill and unfold it as you ask its owner to jot down the number. Hand him the pencil and visiting card and apparently read the number of the bill, really reading the number written on the envelope, which you hold in the same hand beneath the bill. Again fold the bill and put it in the envelope, pushing it half through the slit as shown in Figure 12. Display the bill in this position, your right thumb covering the number written on the flap. Then take the envelope in the left hand, thumb on top and fingers beneath, the fingers covering the slit and the portion of the bill protruding from it, moisten the flap and seal the envelope. Hold the envelope in front of the lighted candle for a moment so that the shadow outline of the bill can be seen against the light, and then lean over and light your cigarette in the flame of the candle. (The cigarette contains enough tobacco to smoke for some time.) As you light the cigarette slide the bill out of the slit in the envelope with your right thumb and hold it behind the right fingers. Then take the envelope with the left hand, leaving the bill concealed in the right, and immediately pick up the match box with the right hand and drop it into your pocket, leaving the bill there also.

Wave the envelope gently above the flame of the candle so as to warm it and then turn to the audience and address them. As you speak to the audience (you must prepare some special talk for this moment) you allow the envelope to be caught in the flame of the candle, as though by accident. You should appear to be in blissful ignorance of the catastrophe which is overtaking the borrowed bill until the flames begin to lick your fingers—and then you panic and pass the flaming envelope from hand to hand in fumbling futility. Finally, in despair, you drop it into the ash tray and watch it burn!

When the laughter has subsided quietly show your hands empty and remove the cigarette from your lips. Quickly tear off the lighted end and drop it into the ash tray, then break open the remainder of the cigarette and unroll the one dollar bill. Check the number of the bill with the record taken of it, and hand it back to its owner (?)!

The bold artifice of reading the number of the duplicate bill when pretending to read the number of the borrowed one may seem at first sight a risky one, but on reflection you will see that the procedure, as we have described it, is absolutely *natural*, and you may always be certain that if your procedure is natural it will never be suspected. Timid souls, however, will never carry off a thing like this—will never read the number with the necessary ease and *je ne sais quoi*—but then, timid souls will never make good conjurers. However, there is another procedure which dispenses with this subterfuge, which dispenses, indeed, with the need for a duplicate bill, and this we will now describe in the trick we will call

THE BILL IN THE EGG

For the first time in this Handbook we shall ask you to visit one of the conjuring shops and make two small purchases costing but very little—a Thumb Tip and a few sheets of Flash Paper.

The Thumb Tip is a little shell of metal or celluloid-compound shaped to fit over the extremity of the thumb and painted " flesh colour " to resemble that digit. The celluloid tips are generally better shaped than the metal ones and fit the thumb better, but, as they are inflammable, there is some danger if they are used in conjunction with fire, as in this case. It is better then to buy a metal one. You will probably think the tip is a very poor imitation of the thumb, especially as to its colour, but this is not important because it should never be seen by the spectators except for a fleeting moment. Its shape and its colour matter very little, the only important thing is that it should not *shine*. So keep it, when it is not in use, in a little box, and do not let it get polished through being carried always in one of your pockets, as some amateurs do. Remember that a shiny thumb tip attracts attention, and that is the very last thing a thumb tip should do.

Flash paper is a commodity of frequent use to the conjurer and is tissue paper which has been impregnated specially. It is very dangerous stuff to make and we shall not describe its manufacture. Once it is made it is quite harmless when handled in small quantities, but it burns away in a flash when touched by a match or a lighted cigarette and, leaving practically no ash, it seems to disappear. For our present purpose you will require a piece about three inches square.

Your other requisites will be a raw egg, a plate, a spoon, a table napkin, a visiting card, and a pencil, all of which should be on your table. A cigarette lighter should be in your right coat pocket. Your thumb tip should be in your trouser pocket by the side of the folded piece of flash paper. It should be mouth upward so that your thumb can be thrust into the tip as you take the paper from the pocket.

If we may now drop into conjurer's jargon for a moment, we would mention that an amusing " gag " is to " plant " the egg with a member of the audience. That is to say, you take an opportunity to speak to one of the audience before your show and ask him to put the egg in his pocket and give it to you when you want it later. You give him very brief instructions, and we will describe the trick as though the egg has been " planted " in this way.

Your first task is to borrow from your audience, as pleasantly as possible, a Bank note; " Any sort of note," you say, " ten dollars, five bucks, a thousand francs, a million chinese dollars,—or one dollar bill." When a bill is offered hand the visiting card and pencil to the owner and ask him, before he parts with his money, to take a note of the number of it, on the card.

While he is doing that say, in quite a normal tone of voice, as if it were a most natural request: " I wonder if someone else will lend me an egg. Will someone oblige me with an egg?" The man who has the egg, following the instructions you gave him, says: " Yes, here you are," in an equally ordinary way. You take the egg from him, thank him, and hand it to another person in the front row of your audience, saying, " Would you mind taking care of this gentleman's egg for a few moments." Done with what comedians call a " dead pan," that is to say, a perfectly straight face, the thing is very funny, and the absurdity of trying and succeeding in borrowing an egg will suddenly smite the audience and draw a peal of laughter.

The other person will by now have made a record of the number of the bill. First retrieve your pencil, do not forget this, and then take the bill and carefully fold it into a little packet small enough to go into the thumb tip. Display this little packet at the tips of the left fingers while your right hand takes the piece of flash paper from the trouser pocket and brings the thumb tip out, in position upon the right thumb, concealed behind the paper.

The paper is now transferred to the left hand, where it is held between the second and third fingers. The right hand

then takes the bill, holding it between the first finger and
the " thumb-tipped " thumb. The left hand folds the flash
paper upwards and the right places the note within the fold.
The left fingers grasp the thumb tip through the paper and
retain it with the bill within the folded paper. The bill
is removed from the paper and shown to the audience once
more—and then returned to the paper, being this time,
pushed into the thumb tip. The right thumb is thrust into
the tip on top of the bill and the tip is withdrawn from the
paper with the bill safely within it. The paper is then
screwed up into a rough bundle as though it contained the
bill, and displayed at the tips of the right first finger and
thumb in such a way that the thumb is immediately behind
the paper packet and the thumb tip is completely screened.
Both hands are held with their palms to the audience to
emphasize the point that the performer holds nothing but
the little packet which contains the borrowed note.

The little packet is now transferred to the left hand while
the right takes out the cigarette lighter and " strikes " it.
The paper packet is gently warmed in the flame of the lighter,
with the disastrous result you will have anticipated. The
packet flares up and disappears.

You stand for a moment in mock confusion and then
say: " I hope you've still got that egg safely." Take the
egg from the person who has been holding it and display it
to the audience with obviously empty hands. Hold the egg
over the plate and break one end with the spoon. Push
your thumb, with the thumb tip, right through the broken
end of the egg, leave the thumb tip inside the egg, and
slowly and deliberately draw out the bill. Put the egg
down and then open the bill and read out the number,
asking the owner of the bill to check with his record.
Return the bill to him and wipe your hands on the napkin.

After the show remember to recover your thumb tip from
the egg and leave behind no evidence to explain your
amusing mystery.

We should like you to notice how, throughout the trick,
you *use* the hand that carries the thumb tip. You use it as

naturally as possible, and quite freely, and the audience will notice nothing peculiar even though you may, at times, fail to completely hide the thumb tip.

To avoid unduly complicating and lengthening our description we have described this trick with a cigarette lighter used to ignite the flash paper, but this is a somewhat mundane method unworthy of a true conjurer. When we have performed the feat we have always used, instead, the little trick of

THE LIGHTED MATCH FROM THE POCKET

The simplest way of taking a lighted match from your pocket is to have a matchbox in the trouser pocket with a loose match lying beside it. You simply rub the match against the box as you remove it from the pocket. But it is sometimes difficult to find the match quickly and without fumbling and it is better to use a special match holder, of which there are various types. You may buy one at a conjuring shop or you may make your own.

To make your own match holder, paste the two sides cut from a match box, end to end, upon a strip of good card (a strip cut from a playing card will do well) and then fold the strip so that the two match box sides are face to face. Fasten a loop of string and a safety pin to the end, place a match between the two striking surfaces and twist a small elastic band around several times to hold the match firmly in place. Pin this little apparatus into the top of your pocket. When the match is pulled out it is ignited by friction against the striking surfaces pressed together by the elastic band.

This holder can, of course, be used to produce a lighted match from other places besides the pocket. It can be hung, for instance, under the edge of your jacket. Renew the striking surfaces from time to time.

The thumb tip you have purchased is an extremely useful little piece of apparatus and we will give you another trick in which it may be used:

THE SMOKE TRICK

It will be, perhaps, an agreeable change to both Author and Reader if we first describe the effect of this trick as the audience will see it and then tackle the " how, why and when " of it all.

The performer produces a cigarette and a lighted match. He lights the cigarette and then extinguishes the match by blowing down his sleeve. He inverts a tumbler upon a saucer and covers it with his pocket handkerchief. He blows clouds of smoke towards the tumbler. He pushes the cigarette into his left fist and makes it disappear. Finally he uncovers the tumbler and shows it to be filled with the smoke of the cigarette.

Let us first take the production of the cigarette and the lighted match. Insert a long pin, point upwards, in the back of the left lapel of your coat and impale a cigarette upon it so that it is concealed behind the lapel. Place the match holder, with a match within it, beneath the bottom edge of your jacket on the right hand side.

Make some remark about wishing to smoke, and place both hands flat upon your jacket pockets as if you were feeling for your cigarette case. The action shows that your hands are empty and calls attention to that fact far better than if you mentioned it, for, in that case the audience might have doubted it. You will find that while it is always necessary to direct the attention of an audience to everything that you wish them to see it is almost invariably better to do so indirectly. If you say: " Observe that my hands are absolutely empty," they will immediately suspect you of concealing something within or behind them. But to return to our trick.

With your hands spread upon your jacket, look down at the bottom edge of it, pause for a moment, and then pull the lighted match out of the holder with your right hand. At the same moment quietly take the cigarette from behind the left lapel with your other hand. Then suddenly turn your head and look at the cigarette. You will find that the action of the left hand will pass unnoticed, all eyes being upon the right hand and the match, and the cigarette will seem to have suddenly appeared in the left hand.

You proceed to light the cigarette and then extinguish the match by blowing down the left sleeve, as we explained in Part I.

The appearance of the smoke in the tumbler is due to chemical means. In the beginning the saucer stands on top of the tumbler. In the saucer are a few drops of liquid ammonia; in the tumbler a few drops of hydrochloric acid. The precise amounts required must be found by experiment, as they depend upon the strength and quality of the chemicals used. (Perhaps we should mention that hydrochloric acid should be handled with care, although the warning may be wasted in these days of technical education.) After lighting your cigarette you lift the saucer and put it down on the table. Then you casually display the glass and invert it on the saucer. As soon as the two chemicals come into contact they begin to form a cloud of white sal ammoniac and moisture smoke. To prevent the formation of the smoke being seen, and the chemical nature of the trick disclosed, you immediately cover the tumbler with your pocket handkerchief.

Behind this handkerchief, in your pocket, rested your thumb tip and, as you took the handkerchief from your pocket, you obtained the tip upon the left thumb. When you have blown a number of clouds of smoke towards the glass, and your cigarette is reduced to half its original length, you double your left thumb into the palm of the hand and close the fingers upon the thumb tip. Then you withdraw the thumb alone, leaving the tip within the left fist. You take the cigarette from your mouth and thrust it, deliberately, lighted end first, into the left fist (and, secretly, into the thumb tip). You insert your right first finger and thumb within the fist as if to extinguish the cigarette and you thrust your thumb into the thumb tip and crush the cigarette within it. The cigarette is quickly extinguished and is then withdrawn, inside the thumb tip, upon the right thumb. The right hand is held with the first finger extended, as if to say: " Attention," and with the second finger tip touching the end of the thumb. The palm is towards the audience and the hand is plainly empty. The action adequately masks the thumb tip while being at once elegant and natural. All this time your eyes watch the left hand, which now begins a little rubbing movement, as though kneading the cigarette away. After a few moments the hand is opened to show that the cigarette has disappeared.

You uncover the glass to reveal the smoke and, in replacing the handkerchief in your pocket, you leave the thumb tip there.

There you have a trick very much in the modern manner . . . . the cigarette produced " from nowhere " and the straightforward presentation without any assistance from the audience. The conjurers who entertained our grandfathers took every opportunity to let members of the audience take part in their tricks and borrowed their properties from the audience instead of producing them from the air.

By way of a change we give you next an old and famous trick called

THE RING ON THE STICK

which is not often seen nowadays but which, in spite of its simplicity, is well worth doing. It is found in the repertoire of nearly all the native Indian conjurers, who do it very well, and the celebrated Charles Bertram (the favourite conjurer of King Edward the Seventh) did not disdain it. You will find, with experience, that the simplest tricks are nearly always the best, their clean cut effects being easily followed, appreciated, and remembered by the audience. It requires a very great deal of experience to present a complicated effect without hopelessly fogging the audience so that they lose track of the course of events and are more muddled than astonished, more bewildered than surprised.

In the old books of magic and conjuring this trick is described with a wand used in place of a stick, but conjurers seldom use a wand today. Technically this is, perhaps, a pity, because the wand was very useful to the old conjurers, who used it very cleverly at times to conceal the presence of an object in the hand. These old conjurers thought nothing of producing an object as large as an orange from grandfather's beard. This is how they managed it. Wherever they performed the old conjurers used their own tables which were fitted with nice little shelves at the back. They called this shelf the *servante* since nearly all the technical terms of the conjuring of that day were French ones. On the *servante* was the orange. On the table itself, its end projecting above the *servante*, was the conjurer's wand, a neat little ebony stick with ivory or silver ends. Very occasionally the ends were real silver. Stepping up to his table the conjurer would scoop up the orange and grasp his wand, and remark that he required an orange. Walking down amongst his audience he would indicate grandfather with a wave of his *empty* hand and say: " Here is a most infinitely obliging gentleman who has had the kindness to bring an orange with him." He would place his wand smartly under his arm and with a " Pardon me, Sir!" would plunge his hand into grandfather's beard and slowly draw out the orange! The family would remember the occasion for forty years. Those were the days!

Instead of a wand you will use a thin stick two or three feet long, and you will also require a large silk handkerchief or scarf in one corner of which you have made a little pocket in which is sewn a cheap ring.

You begin by showing the stick, which you place under your left arm. You then borrow a ring, a man's ring for preference, since it is more easily handled. Holding the ring between the right first finger and thumb you display the silk handkerchief between your hands, the corner containing the dummy ring being clipped between the right middle fingers. You apparently place the ring in the centre of the handkerchief and grasp it through the silk with the left hand. Actually it is the dummy ring in the corner of the handkerchief which you thus hold, the borrowed ring remaining finger-palmed in the right hand. With this hand you take the stick from beneath the left arm, sliding the ring on to the end of the stick as you do so. You will find it will require a fair amount of practice to do this deftly in one action, without any fumbling. You tap the ring through the handkerchief with the stick.

You ask some person to step forward for a moment and hold the ring, and you give it to him to hold through the handkerchief. You slide your hand, with the borrowed ring, along the stick to its centre and hold it horizontally beneath the handkerchief so that the ring is well covered by the hanging folds. You get two other persons to hold the ends of the stick, insisting that they hold it perfectly horizontally. This allows you to keep your hand on the stick and prevent a premature exposure of the ring.

When all is ready you grasp one corner of the handkerchief and, with a quick pull, draw it smartly away so that it brushes against the ring on the stick and sets it spinning, giving an excellent illusion of the ring having just arrived there.

We shall now give you a trick which has the appearance of requiring considerable dexterity while, in reality, it requires nothing more than neatness in palming or finger-palming. The properties are simple: three tumblers, a cone of stiff red paper, a cone of stiff white paper, a cone of stiff blue paper, and nine table tennis balls, three of which have been painted red, three blue, and the other three left white. After this narration of colours you will not be surprised to know that the trick is called

THE PATRIOTIC BALLS

The paper cones are simply twisted sheets of stout coloured paper, and they are stood in three tumblers, in a row, with the points of the cones towards the audience. The balls are arranged on the table in front of the cones, each set of three balls before the cone of the same colour.

The trick may be presented as an observation test, the audience being asked to observe all your actions closely and to try to state, at the conclusion, the position of the balls. The conjurer apparently puts the three red balls into the red cone, the white into the white one, and the blue into the blue one, but when the cones are inverted a red, a white, and a blue ball roll out of each.

The following series of movements will bring about this result:

1. Take a red ball and pretend to put it into the red cone but, as soon as your hand is behind the point of the cone, finger palm the ball and flip the inside of the cone with your fingers to simulate the sound of the ball dropping into it.

2. Pretend to put a white ball into the white cone, but let the finger palmed red ball drop in instead, and finger palm the white one in its place.

3. Pretend to put a blue ball into the blue cone, but drop the finger palmed white one instead, and palm the blue one.

4. Pretend to put a second red ball into the red cone, but really drop the palmed blue one and palm the red one in its place.

5. Actually drop a white ball into the white cone (still keeping the red ball palmed).

6. Pretend to put a second blue ball into the blue cone, but really palm it and drop the red one instead.

7. Actually put a red ball into the red cone (keeping the blue ball palmed).

8. Pretend to put a white ball into the white cone but drop the blue instead.

9. Actually drop the last blue ball into the blue cone, keeping the second blue ball palmed.

10. Grasp the red cone by its top, the fingers, and the finger palmed blue ball, inside the cone, lift it out of the tumbler in which it stands and turn it over so that the balls roll out, letting the palmed blue ball roll out with the red and the white.

11. Invert the white cone in the same way, showing red, white, and blue balls.

12. Do the same with the blue cone.

A program of magic should have plenty of variety, and after a sleight-of-hand trick you can very well follow with one using a certain amount of apparatus, such as

THE CELEBRITY TRICK

which we will now describe.

This is how the audience will see it. The performer first shows, one by one, nine postcard photographs of celebrated persons, which he gives to one of the company to hold. An ordinary photograph frame is then shown, and taken to pieces, demonstrating that it contains, simply, a back, a glass, and two sheets of white card. The frame is re-assembled, wrapped in a sheet of brown paper, and given to another spectator for safe keeping. A packet of small cards, each bearing the name of one of the celebrities, is dropped into a little bag and shaken up. One of the cards is drawn from the bag. The portrait of the celebrity whose name appears upon the chosen card disappears from the batch of postcards and reappears in the frame.

The trick is capable of a good deal of variation to suit the tastes of different audiences. It need not be confined to portraits of celebrities but all kinds of pictures may be used. There are three things to consider: the disappearance of the postcard, its reappearance in the frame, and the " choice " of the celebrity. We have written " choice " in quotation marks because we think you may have guessed that it is a question of " Hobson's choice."

The disappearance of the postcard is brought about by four minute pellets of wax on the back of one of the other portraits. A special " conjurers' wax " can be purchased from the conjuring shops which is admirable for this purpose, but a soft beeswax, or even ordinary soap, will do very well. Place the card that is to disappear fourth in the pile of postcards and the card with the wax pellets upon its back, third. Show the cards one by one, counting them, calling the names, and dropping them face downwards on to your table. The one that is to disappear will thus fall face down upon the wax pellets. Pick the cards up, place an elastic band around them, and hand them to the assisting member of the audience, squeezing them together as you do so, to make the card adhere to its waxed neighbour. When, later, you count and display the cards again, by dealing them one by one on to your table, the double card will be dealt as if it were one, and the " vanish " will be accomplished. The elastic band placed round the packet of cards will effectively keep a meddlesome assistant from looking through it.

The frame in which the portrait reappears is quite unprepared and any frame with a removable back may be used. The frame contains two pieces of white card upon one of which a duplicate of the postcard that is to vanish is mounted. At the beginning the cards are in the frame with the portrait in between them. There is also, unknown to the spectators, a third piece of white card just large enough to fit in to the front of the frame. This piece of card is covered on one side by a piece of thin transparent celluloid and on the other side with a piece of brown paper to match the paper in which the frame is brought forward. In performance the brown paper parcel is placed upon the table and opened. The frame is picked up and shown, the celluloid fake being left lying upon the paper, where, because of its brown paper backing, it rests unperceived. The frame is put down upon the paper and taken to pieces. First the back is shown, then the two white cards together, then the glass, and, finally, the frame itself. In reassembling the frame the white cards are replaced separately, the one bearing the portrait being replaced first, with the portrait looking through the glass, then the second card is replaced, and finally the back. The frame is then picked up *with the celluloid fake in front of it*, and shown. The celluloid resembles the glass and the fake makes the frame appear to be still empty. The frame is then wrapped in the paper again and given to someone to hold for a while. Later the frame is taken from the paper (leaving the fake lying face down and imperceptible upon it) and is shown with the portrait in place.

We must now explain how it happens that the portrait is always the one selected, how the selection is " forced," as conjurers say. The little bag in which the cards are shaken up is not so simple as it seems, being, in fact, divided into two compartments by a partition across its width. It should be about nine inches square and be made of fairly thick material such as stout flannel, for example. In one of the two compartments are nine cards each bearing the name of the same celebrity it is desired to " force." The cards which the conjurer displays, bearing different names, number only *eight*, and there is no card amongst them bearing the name which will be forced. These cards are dropped into the empty compartment of the bag and the bag is thoroughly shaken. In presenting the bag to the spectator it is held so that the compartment holding the different names is closed and the "selection" is made from the cards which are all alike. When the card has been drawn the conjurer thrusts his hand into the bag, takes out eight " all different " cards and tosses them on to the table. The bag he folds up and puts aside.

It only remains to consider the presentation. An important thing to remember when performing a trick of this kind before an audience of any size, is to get the people who will assist to do so upon the platform, where they can be seen by all the others. Avoid going down into your audience, especially in a large hall. You will begin, therefore, if performing in a hall, by asking for two people to step upon the stage to assist you. In a performance before a small company it will be sufficient to ask two people to draw their chairs forward where they can be seen readily by all the company. Then you display the postcards, count them, call the names, place the elastic band around them and hand them to one of the assistants, pressing them firmly together as you do so.

Next you open your brown paper parcel and show the frame. You undo the frame, show all the parts, and re-assemble it. You show it once more, apparently empty, wrap it up in the paper again, and hand it to the second assistant to hold.

You then display the small cards bearing the names and allow the assistants to see that they are all different. But you must NOT ask them to notice this point. To mention that the cards are all different would be to suggest to them the possibility of cards being all alike, which is the last thought you desire to put into their heads! Drop the cards into the bag, shake them up, and have one " selected," asking the chooser to conceal the name from you for the moment. Remove the eight different cards from the bag, show them to the assistant, the name on the top one showing, and say to him, " I am glad you did not chose So-and-So." (*Oh, wicked, wicked* !) Place cards and bag aside.

Take the postcards from the assistant and ask him to announce the name of the celebrity he has chosen. Make a " pass," as impressively as you are able to, from the post-cards towards the frame, and then count the cards on to the table, calling their names as you do so. The selected card has vanished!

Take the brown paper parcel from the other assistant, place it on your table and undo it. Pick up the frame and show it to the spectators, with the selected protrait successfully within.

Should you feel indisposed to use so much " apparatus " as the frame we have described, you may substitute for it

THE NEST OF ENVELOPES

making the selected postcard pass into the innermost of a nest of three. The procedure appears to be very fair. The performer shows a large envelope. Opening it he removes a second envelope, considerably smaller. Inside that, in turn, is a third one, just large enough to hold a postcard. This envelope he hands to a spectator to inspect and seal. After putting the spectator's initials upon this smallest envelope the performer seals it in the larger which, in turn, he encloses within the largest. In spite of all this the chosen postcard passes into the sealed and initialed envelope.

The secret lies in a fourth envelope, a duplicate of the smallest one, already sealed, with the second postcard within it. This extra envelope lies with its duplicate within the one of middle size. The envelopes should be of good quality, perfectly opaque, and each one a good deal larger than the one intended to go inside it.

In performance you open the nest and hand a spectator the smallest envelope, asking him to examine and seal it. You take it from him and slide it into the larger one, but immediately check yourself and draw it half out again. You will recognize the " afterthought " again and realize that it is the duplicate envelope containing the postcard which is drawn out this time. You ask the spectator for his initials which you write in bold letters upon the envelope, which you then seal within the larger one.

When, later, you open the nest of envelopes, you take care to hand the spectator the correct one and ask him to verify the initials upon it!

You will have to spend another quarter or two at a conjuring shop before you can do our next trick, one of the " classics " known in England as The Egg and the Handkerchief and in America by the more distinctive title of

KLING KLANG

because of the sound the egg makes against the sides of a tumbler into which it is placed in the course of the trick. You will need two of the small silk handkerchiefs conjurers use, each fifteen inches square, and a bottomless tumbler. A bottomless tumbler is not, as you might suppose, a drinker's dream of unlimited " booze," but a tumbler from which the bottom has been removed with a glass cutter so that, unlike most tumblers, it has both an entrance and an exit. We suggest that you use white silk handkerchiefs so that you can wear one in your coat pocket as if it were an ordinary article. Actually, conjurer's handkerchiefs are made from thin Japanese silk, or imitation silk, and have very small hems, so that they can be folded or compressed into a very small amount of space. You will also need a real egg, a table tennis ball in the side of which you must cut a half inch hole, and a cylinder of stout paper or cardboard large enough to go over your bottom-less tumbler and about two inches taller. Pasted inside this cylinder at one end is a small tube just sufficiently large to hold the second silk handkerchief when it has been care-fully folded and pleated into a small parcel. All this is illustrated in Fig. 13.

Folded Silk
Handkerchief
in Inner Tube

Ball with
hole inside
FIG 13

In the beginning the bottomless tumbler, covered by the cardboard cylinder and with one of the silk handkerchiefs packed into the inner tube, is on your table. The second silk handkerchief is in your breast pocket with the table tennis ball behind it. The hole in the ball is uppermost so that when you take the handkerchief from your pocket you can slip the tip of your second finger into the ball and bring it out of the pocket behind the silk. The egg is in your right coat pocket where you can easily obtain and palm it in your right hand. Simply let it lie within the half closed fingers.

You can begin the trick by producing the egg from beneath a boy's chin just as the old conjurer used to produce the orange from grandfather's whiskers, as we described in " The Ring on the Stick." Read our description of that feat again and remember to reach out first with the left hand, so as to attract the attention of the spectators to that hand, and then produce the egg with the other one.

Now remove the cardboard cylinder and casually display the tumbler, holding it with the hand cupped around the base so that the fingers mask its bottomless condition. With the glass held thus, tilt it sideways and slide the egg into it. Rock the glass so that the egg taps against the slides and produces the characteristic " Kling, klang." Pick up the cardboard cylinder and drop it over the tumbler as the latter stands upon your hand. Lift the cylinder an inch or two to show the egg once more and, as you replace it, push the folded silk out of the inner tube with your forefinger, so that it falls into the tumbler on top of the egg. Now grasp the cylinder from the outside, gripping the tumbler through the sides of it, and pick up both together. The egg slides through the bottom of the glass and rests on the left fingers which simultaneously close a little to hide and to finger palm it. The back of the left hand is turned towards the spectators as the right hand carries tumbler and cylinder away and puts them on the table. There is no real difficulty about the manoeuvre, but it must be practiced assiduously to get the correct TIMING.

You now draw the white silk handkerchief from your pocket, bringing out the table tennis ball also, on the tip of the second finger. You bend the second finger inwards and place the ball in the right palm. You then wave the silk handkerchief in the air, keeping the back of the hand always towards the audience, and work the handkerchief gently into the ball with the tips of the second and third fingers. If this is well done the handkerchief will appear to gradually diminish and fade away as it is waved in the air. When the silk handkerchief is almost totally within the ball you bring the left hand up to the right and put the egg in front of the ball. You open the hands slightly to show the egg, keeping the ball behind it, then grip the ball in the left palm and drop that hand to the side again, leaving the egg in the right hand. Display the egg freely and then hand it to one of the spectators, who will be surprised to find that it is a real one.

Turn back to your table, lift the cylinder, and show the handkerchief in the tumbler. Replace the handkerchief in your breast pocket and, as you do so, drop the table tennis ball into one of the other pockets.

It is rather a pity that one very seldom sees, nowadays, a trick with a borrowed ring, and we give you next a modernized version of an old trick that is at once extremely effective and full of humour. We will call it

THE LOST RING

The performer begins by giving to a member of the audience for " safe custody " a box which he calls his " jewel box." It is simply a cardboard box tied up with red tape. He then borrows a ring from one of the ladies, which he wraps in a square of tissue paper, and warms with a lighted match, as he announces his intention of passing it into the " jewel box." There is a sudden flash of fire and the paper disappears—the ring also. Opening the " jewel box " the performer takes from it a matchbox, inside which, he says, is the lady's ring. Opening the box he takes out a little paper parcel within which is a ring with a huge " emerald," which he offers to the lady but which she promptly disowns. He replaces this ring in the matchbox and takes another from the " jewel box." This matchbox proves to contain a ring with a huge " ruby " which the lady also refuses to acknowledge as hers. All the matchboxes in the " jewel case " are opened in turn, revealing an astonishing collection of " magnificent jewelry " . . . . but not the lady's ring! The boxes are placed together on the table and one is chosen by the audience by a process of elimination. This box is opened by the lady and in it she finds her ring.

We will now describe the various properties and their disposal. The collection of imitation rings *may* be dispensed with but it adds much humour to the trick and without it the business of showing the matchboxes empty would be very tedious. The rings can be obtained, either from a five and dime store, or a costume jewelry shop, and you will need ten of them, as preposterous as possible. You wrap each one in tissue paper and put it into an empty matchbox. These, in turn, you put into an ordinary cardboard box which you tie round with red tape. In your right trouser pocket you place an eleventh matchbox with its drawer half open, and in the upper part of this same pocket you fasten the little holder for the production of a lighted match which we described on an earlier page.

You next take three pieces of flash paper, each about three inches square. One of these pieces you roll into a tight " wick "and twist into a circle. You then wrap it in one of the other pieces to make a little dummy packet which will roughly resemble a ring wrapped in paper. You put this dummy packet into a convenient pocket with the third piece of flashpaper, and you are ready to perform.

You first give the " jewel box " to some one to hold and then you ask for the loan of a ring. You take out your little piece of flash paper and also the dummy packet, and hold them in your left hand with the dummy underneath, unseen. You take the ring and place it on the piece of paper which you fold around it to make a packet like the dummy one. You transfer both packets to the right hand, turning them over as you do so to bring the real packet underneath the dummy. Then you put the dummy packet *alone* back into the left hand while your right hand goes *without haste* into your trouser pocket. You put the ring packet into the matchbox, close the box, and then pull the lighted match from the pocket. With this you flash off the dummy packet . . . . and the ring has disappeared!

You ask the man who holds the box if he heard the ring arrive within it and, while talking to him, you casually put your hand into your pocket and finger palm the matchbox. Taking the " jewel box " from the holder of it you put it on your table *and leave the palmed matchbox behind it.*

You now open the box and remove the matchboxes, one by one, displaying the contents and asking the lender of the ring if each one is hers. You can get a great deal of fun from this, especially when she disowns a particularly gawdy monstrosity and you ask her if she is *quite sure* it is not her ring. After showing each ring you replace it in its matchbox and you toss the boxes carelessly upon the table by the side of the " jewel box." When all the rings have been shown you pick up the " jewel box " and place it aside, and the eleventh matchbox which was behind it is thus, imperceptibly and easily, added to the others.

You now ask the lady if she is sure she would not like to have one of the rings in exchange for her own! When she refuses you ask if she would take half the rings for hers and you divide the matchboxes into two heaps, one of five and one of six, taking care that the box with the borrowed ring (of which you must never lose sight) is one of the five.

Turn to the man who held the " jewel box " and ask him to choose one of the heaps, " this one or that." If he chooses the heap of six say, " Good. We will put those back then," and pick them up and drop them into the " jewel box." But if he chooses the heap of five you say, " Very good, we shall not need the others then," and still you pick up the heap of six and drop them into the box.

The five remaining boxes you arrange in two sets, of two boxes and three boxes, the borrowed ring in one of the two, and say, " Which now, two or three?" If he replies " Three," you gather them up and drop them into the " jewel box," then you pick up the other two and hand them to him. But if he replies " Two " you simply pick up the two boxes and hand them to him, asking him to hold one box in each hand and noting with which hand he holds the box that contains the borrowed ring. (You may have this box marked, if you wish, in some inconspicuous way, but so that you can always recognize it.)

You turn to the lady and ask her to choose one of the boxes the gentleman holds. If she chooses the one that does not contain her ring you take it from the man and toss it into the " jewel box " and ask him to open the other one. If, on the other hand, she chooses the box that *does* contain her ring, you ask the man to hand it to her and allow her to open it herself and recover her property.

Thus all ends happily, whichever way they choose, by means of the famous " conjurer's choice " of which you should make a careful note, for it can be used in many other ways in many other tricks.

After the expense to which we put them in the last trick our readers, especially those inclined to thrift, will welcome a trick which costs practically nothing. It is a trick with paper that is probably of Japanese origin but which, for some inexplicable reason is always called

THE AFGHAN BANDS

The performer shows a long strip of paper the ends of which have been pasted together to form a band or ring. He cuts the ring, lengthwise with a pair of scissors, cutting right round the circle and making of it, as might be expected, two separate bands. He does exactly the same thing with a second band but calls the attention of the audience to the fact that this time he utters a magic word as he cuts the band, with the result that, instead of two single bands, he makes two which are linked to each other. He cuts a third band in the same way, but this time he utters a different word, and at the conclusion of the cutting he has one long band. The three results obtained are illustrated at A, B, and C in Fig. 14.

The secret lies entirely in the fabrication of the bands which are made from strips of newspaper about two inches wide and at least four feet long. The first band, which divides into two equal rings, is exactly what it appears to be, a plain straightforward ring. But in joining the second band one end of the paper strip is turned over, *once*, before it is pasted to the other end. In joining the third band one end is turned over *twice* before it is fastened. Provided the

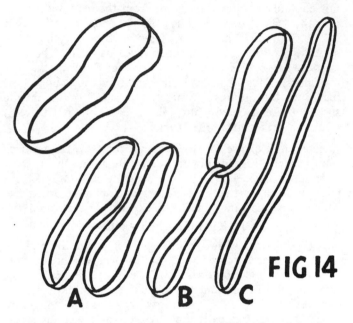

FIG 14

A   B   C

bands are not too short the twists will not be noticed . . . which is why we have given you the minimum length of four feet.

As to the magic words, you will find two old favourites, ABRACADABRA and ALDIBORONTICOFOSCOFORNIO, as effective today as ever they have been.

We come now to a trick of a very different kind, of a kind of conjuring which has become rather popular of late years under the general name of " mental magic," the devotees of which call themselves " mentalists," an unhappy choice which, always, irresistibly reminds this writer of mental institutions. We will call the trick

THE MYSTERIOUS ADDITION

It is a trick that can be accomplished in many different ways and presented, also, to produce different effects. We will describe it to you, first, as a prediction effect.

First the performer writes a prediction upon a scrap of paper, which he folds and leaves in some prominent place. Four members of the audience each give him a four figure number, which he writes upon a piece of paper, a card, or a scribbling pad. A fifth member of the audience adds the column of figures so formed. The prediction is opened and read, and found to tally with the total of the sum.

Exactly the same procedure can be used to present the trick as an experiment in mental control, instead of a prediction. The performer declares himself able to control the thoughts of the persons he selects, so that they are compelled to give him the numbers he wills them to, numbers which eventually add to the total he has already written.

The reader is, by this time, sufficiently acquainted with our subject to realize that the total is " forced " in some way. Actually the figures given to the fifth person to add are not those dictated by the first four but another set of figures previously written by the performer, and the total of which he knows. There are various ways of achieving this result.

One method is to have a pad of small sheets of paper or a pile of small cards. You write your sum, the total of which you will predict, on the bottom card or sheet of paper. The figures furnished by the spectators are written upon the top card. As you approach the fifth person you turn your pad, or pile of cards, over, so as to bring the prepared figures uppermost, and hand the new top card, or piece of paper, to the fifth person for addition.

Another method is to have a little bundle of slips of paper held together by a broad rubber band. The figures given by the spectators are written upon the pad as shown in Fig. 15, two lines being drawn beneath them. The piece of paper is then removed from the pad and handed to

Half Sheet

FIG 15

someone for the addition of the figures. The secret lies in the fact that the top sheet, upon which the figures have been written, is only half a sheet. It is held in place by the rubber band, which also conceals its bottom edge. This half sheet hides the performer's own figures, which are written on the top half of the second sheet. It is upon this second sheet that the two lines for the total are drawn. The left thumb holds the half sheet in position while the right hand grasps the bottom of the second sheet and draws it off the pad.

A third method, which we believe was originated by the Author of this book, and has never been published before, is to write the four sets of figures on the margin of a newspaper, which is then torn off and handed to the fifth spectator for the figures to be totalled. The performer's figures, which add to the total he intends to " predict," are first written in the bottom margin of page two of the paper. The spectators' figures are written, as they are given, in the *side* margin at the bottom of page one. The corner is then torn off the paper. This corner will bear both sums, one on each side, as illustrated in Figs. 16 and 17. The

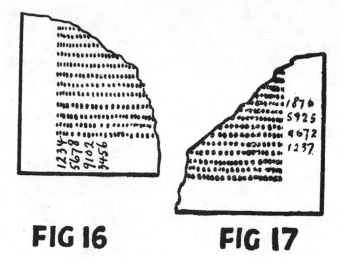

FIG 16   FIG 17

margin bearing the performer's figures is torn off and given for addition while the rest of the corner is carelessly crumpled up and flicked into the fire or dropped into the performer's pocket. The use of a newspaper to jot down the figures gives an appearance of improvisation which is particularly disarming.

Frequently used in conjunction with the last trick is another called

THE SLATE TRICK

in which words, figures, or designs, appear mysteriously upon a slate previously shown void of any kind of inscription. This is a trick which was once very generally used by spurious spirit mediums (*on dit*) and was " adopted " by conjurers. Although slates have long since ceased to be used by any one else they still figure at times in conjuring performances.

There are many methods of making writing appear upon a slate, far too many for us to discuss them at all fully in this Handbook. We will content ourselves with giving you one or two of the best methods with a " flap " slate. This is a slate fitted with a sheet of slate coloured cardboard or plastic which lies within the frame and can therefore cover anything written upon the slate itself. A flap slate may be purchased at a conjuring shop for a few quarters or a few dollars. The expensive models have flaps which " lock " within the frames and can be given for examination by the audience. The cheap models are made throughout of cardboard. Something in betweeen the two is really needed, such as one made of real slate, with a plastic flap, for instance.

The commonest method of using the slate is to write upon it the words or figures which are to appear and to conceal the writing with a flap which has been covered on one side with newspaper. The slate is first shown blank on both sides. A sheet is then torn from a newspaper and the slate is wrapped in it. But, before wrapping, it is put down for a moment upon the rest of the newspaper and, when it is picked up again, it is taken *without the flap*, which is left lying upon the newspaper, unperceived because of the piece of paper pasted on its back.

Another procedure is to put the writing upon the *flap* and to add this to the slate when wrapping it up. Each procedure has its own strong points; in one the slate may be handed to the audience *after* the appearance of the writing and in the other it may be examined *before* the writing appears.

Another procedure is to use with the slate a large " window " envelope, that is to say, an envelope with a large opening cut in its face as shown in Fig. 18. The envelope should be just large enough to contain the slate, and the back of the flap is covered with a piece of paper cut from the front of another similar envelope. The words or figures required are written upon the slate and covered by the flap. In presentation the slate is shown and the initials of a spectator are written upon the slate, not, of course, upon the flap side. The slate is then put into the envelope. The spectators see the slate slide into the envelope

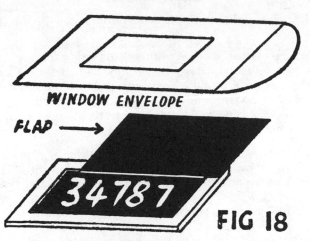

FIG 18

and the initials are plainly in view all the time through the " window." After some hocus pocus the slate is drawn out of the envelope and the flap is left within it, where, because of the matching paper upon its back, it cannot be seen.

Naturally the reverse procedure may also be used. The flap may be in the envelope at the start, unnoticed because of the paper upon its back matching the inside of the envelope. The flap bears the figures or words to be produced. The slate may be inspected by the audience and then put into the envelope, to be withdrawn later with the flap in position.

You will understand that when the Slate Trick is done in conjunction with " The Mysterious Addition " the presentation must be altered. It is no longer a question of a prediction but of the production of mysterious writing revealing an unknown total. You would first show your slate and wrap it up or put it into the envelope, not forgetting to put with it a small piece of chalk. Spirits cannot write without writing implements. Then you will get your figures written and give them to someone to total. That person will be asked to concentrate all his mind upon the total reach ed, which will then be " precipitated " upon the slate.

There is another method of producing slate writing which uses two ordinary slates without any flap, but as it can also be used to produce figures or writing on ordinary pieces of cardboard, and as we think this procedure much to be preferred, we will describe it in that form, dubbing it, for identification,

THE INVISIBLE SCRIBE

This trick can be presented in conjunction with " The Mysterious Addition " or a name may be forced with counters, as we described in " The Celebrity Trick." We would also mention another procedure for forcing a two figure number, such as forty-four. You hand a piece of paper to one of the spectators and ask him to write on it a single figure. You take the paper from him and hand it to another person, asking him to write a second figure beneath the first. As you take the paper from this person you glance at the two figures and mentally add them together . . . . let us say they are eight and six, totalling fourteen. You pass the paper to a third person who, we will suppose writes a five, making the total nineteen. A fifth writes nine, bringing the total to twenty-eight, and a sixth adds another eight, making it thirty-six. As this is less than nine short of the total you require you stop, because the addition of another number might exceed your figure, and say " I will ask someone else to total these figures " and, apparently, you simply draw two lines beneath them and hand the paper to another person. Actually, however, you quickly add an eight to the column of figures, to make the forty-four you want, and then draw the lines beneath it for the last spectator to insert the total.

We will now return to the pieces of cardboard upon which we shall produce our writing. They may be as small as postcards or as large as posters, but we will suggest pieces about the size of a sheet of business writing paper.

Both sides of the cards should have the same appearance. With a blue crayon pencil write the figure 44 boldly upon one of the cards and in the top left hand corner of it write a small, but not too small figure 1. Place this card on top of the other with the writing face downward and put a rubber band round the cards to hold them securely.

If you will follow our description with two cards, or even two pieces of paper, in your hands, you will understand it more easily. Pick up the two cards and show them on both sides and remove the rubber band. Take the top card and place it underneath the other, taking care not to allow the spectators to catch sight of the figures written on the underneath side of the card. In the upper left hand corner of the card that is now uppermost write the figure 1 with your blue pencil and show it to the spectators. Grasp the card by its left hand bottom corner, lift it, turn it over, and slide it beneath the other card. Write the figure two in the upper left hand corner of the card that is now on top and show it to the spectators. Grasp this card also by its left hand bottom corner, lift it, turn it over, and slide it beneath the other card, taking care that the figures on one side of it are not seen. Write the figure three in the upper left hand corner of the card now on top, and show it to the spectators. Grasp this card in the same way by its left hand bottom corner, lift it, and turn it over *without sliding it beneath the other card*. Alter the 1 that is written in the upper left hand corner of the card now on top into a 4, and show it to the spectators. Now spread the two cards a little so that the 1 on the corner of the bottom card can also be seen. Then turn the cards over and show the 2 and 3 on the opposite corners. Square up the cards, place the rubber band around them, and hand them to someone to hold.

Proceed with the writing of the figures on the piece of paper and their addition. Ask for the total and, taking your blue pencil, pretend to write the number in the air above the cards. Remove the elastic band and reveal the appearance of the total on the card.

This business of mysterious writing upon slates naturally brings to mind another trick said to have once been popular with fraudulent mediums and generally called

THE BILLET READING TRICK

We will give you a method suitable for presentation by a conjurer.

A number of small pieces of paper are handed round the audience with the request that very brief questions be written upon them. The writers are asked to write their initials plainly beneath their questions and to fold their papers into four with the writing inside. The slips are collected and shaken up in a hat and the performer, taking them out one by one and holding them to his forehead, " divines " the initials of the writers and answers their questions.

The slips of paper should be about two and a half inches long and two inches wide. The paper should be fairly stout and each slip should be previously folded into four and unfolded again. The writers of the questions, when they fold their papers, will naturally follow the original folds, and all the papers will be of the same size and of the same general appearance.

If you will take a slip of paper of the size we have indicated and fold it into four you will find that, if you clip it between your first and second finger tips by the corner that is actually the centre of the paper, you can open the paper *completely* with one movement, by inserting the tip of the thumb beneath one thickness of paper at the opposite corner and pressing the paper flat against the fingers. The illustration, Fig. 19, should make this quite clear . . . the tip of the right thumb is just about to be thrust beneath the uppermost corner of the folded paper, at the point marked X. This movement of opening the paper with one hand must be practised until it can be done very quickly and very surely.

As the performer collects the folded papers from the writers of them, who are asked to drop them into the hat

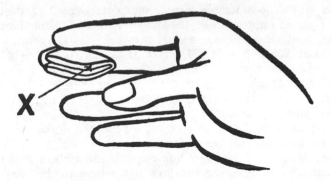

FIG 19

themselves, he shakes the hat vigorously to mix them up. When nearly all the slips have been collected he shakes the hat a little too vigorously, so that some of the slips are shaken right out. He picks the slips up and drops them back into the hat, but, in doing so, he quickly opens one of them with the movement described above and leaves it, open, in the bottom of the hat. As he collects the remaining slips he takes the opportunity to read the writing on the opened slip.

Returning to the platform he puts the hat upon his table and takes from it one of the slips (not the one he has opened) and holds it to his forehead. He asks the writers of the various questions to concentrate their minds upon them. Closing his eyes he begins, as dramatically as possible, to " divine " the initials on the slip, actually naming those written upon the open slip within the hat. He is careful, however, not to be too certain of them, nor does he next give the words of the question but takes care to reply to it somewhat indirectly so as not to give the impression that he reads the actual question.

Let us suppose, for instance, that the initials on the slip lying open in the hat are " H.V.J." and the question itself is " Who will win the Boat Race?" The performer, with an air of considerable strain, says something like this: "I get an impression of the initials H and . . . something not quite clear . . . and a . . . . is it a J? . . . Concentrate please! Would it be H.Y.J.? No! H.V.J.! . . Is that right? Thank you. Concentrate on your question please. Something to do with water isn't it? I see a newspaper head-line . . . it reads, ' Cambridge's Great Victory ' . . . Does that answer your question?" . . .

At that point he opens his eyes, removes the slip of paper from his forehead, opens it, glances at it as if to verify his answer, and nods to himself with satisfaction as he carelessly crumples the slip and drops it on to the floor.

But in that brief moment he has memorized the initials and the question written upon that slip. He can now take another one from the hat and reply to it in the same impressive way. He repeats this process with three or four slips, each time answering the slip he has just read while holding another to his forehead. Finally, he brings from the hat the slip he first read, quickly folding it as he does so, and having apparently read that question also, he drops it to the floor with the others.

Generally the performer only reads a proportion of the questions, excusing himself from reading more because of the " great strain of concentration." The number of slips that are actually read will depend upon the character of the audience and the amount of interest they show in the effect.

Another trick of a similar type is one we will describe under the title of

AUTOMATIC WRITING

You may have assisted in experiments in this kind of thing, which, at one time, was quite a popular fad. If not you may try one now. Place a sheet of paper upon the table before you and rest the point of your pencil upon it, as though to write, but do not let your wrist or forearm rest upon the table. Close your eyes and try to dismiss all thought from your mind and make it an absolute blank. After a while the pencil point will move, involuntarily, and begin to trace meaningless doodles upon the paper. This is as far as the Author has ever got but more . . . shall we say more gifted people sometimes succeed in producing more or less legible writing which, with the interpretation of a vivid imagination, may give a more or less intelligent message!

But we need not here discuss the fact or fallacy of automatic writing, we will simply use it for the *mise en scene* of an ingenious trick, the reproduction by alleged automatic writing of a word written upon a piece of paper by a spectator.

Upon a piece of paper about three inches square the performer draws a circle which he calls a " circle of influence." He asks one of the spectators to write within the circle the name of any famous person, living or dead, and then to fold the paper into four. He takes the folded paper, tears it into pieces, drops the pieces into an ash tray, and sets fire to them. While he tells the audience of the remarkable results to be obtained by automatic writing he holds the point of his pencil in the smoke of the burning paper. Then, after a false attempt, he succeeds in writing the same name upon a small scribbling pad.

Take a piece of paper of the size we have described (about three inches square) draw a circle in the centre of it, and fold the paper twice. If you now tear the folded paper, first into halves and then into quarters, you will find that practically the whole of the circle and, consequently, the name written within it, will be left upon one of the quarters. All the secret of the trick is there. When you receive the folded paper from the writer of the name, you hold the centre portion, which bears the circle, between the right first finger and thumb. You tear the paper into halves, place the left hand piece upon the right, and tear again. It is then a simple matter to clip the centre portion between the tips of the first and second fingers and to drop all the other pieces into the ash tray.

In your right hand pocket you have a small scribbling pad and a box of matches. You put your hand into your pocket and quickly open the centre of the paper and leave it against the face of the pad. You bring out the box of matches and set fire to the pieces in the ash tray.

You hold your pencil in the smoke from the burning paper for a moment and then you take the pad from your pocket, with your right thumb holding the opened centre piece against the face of the pad. You quickly read the name within the circle and then you close your eyes and hold your pencil to the pad. After a moment you make a few convulsive scribbles upon the paper. You open your eyes, look at your " writing " and shake your head. You tear the scribbled sheet from the pad and crumple it up *with the written corner within it* and drop it into your pocket. You ask the writer of the word to concentrate more deeply upon it and you make another attempt, this time producing a scribble which can just be deciphered as the word that was written.

Practice to see how badly you can write the word and still make it just painfully legible, unless you are like some of the Author's friends whose handwriting is always like that.

To return to a simpler type of conjuring, we will give you now a very effective little trick which we will call

THE TRANSPOSED HANDKERCHIEF

The effect of this trick is that the conjurer empties the matches from an ordinary box of " safeties " which he encircles with a rubber band and places in a prominent position. He tucks a small silk handkerchief into his hand, from whence it vanishes, passing invisibly into the match box.

There you have a small trick which has all the elements of success: it is simple in effect and easily followed by the audience and it uses ordinary everyday objects with which they are familiar.

You will need a piece of special equipment called a " Handkerchief pull." This is a sort of egg shaped cup, generally made of aluminium, open at one end, attached to a length of cord elastic. It is worn hanging under the coat beneath the left arm, the elastic passing through the left armhole of the vest and then round the wearer's back, to be fastened to one of the trouser braces in front of the right side. The length of elastic must be adjusted so that the cup of the pull will lie, when it is released, beneath the coat about six inches below the armhole of the vest.

In your left pocket you put two matchboxes, one half full of matches and the other containing one of the white silk handkerchiefs which you used in the trick, " Kling Klang," which we have already taught you. The second handkerchief you wear in your breast pocket. The two matchboxes should lie in your pocket so that you can take them both out together with the one containing the matches on top. In your right coat pocket you have a small rubber band.

You begin by taking the two matchboxes from your pocket and holding them in your left hand in such a manner that the box containing the silk handkerchief is concealed, partly by the other box and partly by the fingers surrounding it. To make the concealment more complete you push the drawer of the upper box half open, showing the matches. Fig. 20 shows the position in which the boxes are held

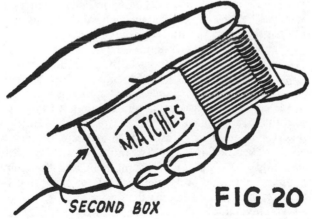

SECOND BOX   FIG 20

and how well the second box is concealed beneath the first. With the boxes held in this position you pull out the matches and drop them on to the table, and then, with your right hand, you close the box. Naturally, you do this by putting your thumb against one end and your fingers against the opposite end and squeezing it shut. The back of the hand and fingers completely hide the box for a moment. As the box shuts, the tips of the right thumb and fingers close upon the concealed box, and both boxes are raised a little so that the lower one now occupies the position in the hand previously taken by the upper one. Without making any attempt to palm the top box, but simply holding it by its ends between fingers and thumb, the hand moves straight to the right coat pocket, leaves the box there, and comes back with the elastic band. To the audience the conjurer appears to have simply closed the box and then taken the rubber band from his pocket. The band is put round the box, lengthwise of course, and the box stood somewhere where it is in full view.

You now stand with your left side turned a little away from the audience and rest your left fist upon your hip. With your right hand you take the silk handkerchief from your breast pocket, toss it into the air, and catch it. While all eyes follow the handkerchief your left hand moves up a few inches, grasps the cup of the pull, and returns to its former position, fist on hip. You now turn to face the audience and bring your left hand in front of you at natural height and begin to tuck the silk handkerchief into it. Actually, of course, you push the silk handkerchief into the cup of the pull. When the silk handkerchief is completely within the cup you release the latter, allowing it to fly back beneath the coat, pulled by the elastic cord. But you continue for a moment or two the movement of tucking the silk handkerchief into the fist and you raise the latter shoulder high. You pause for a moment and then blow gently upon your hand and open it slowly to show that the silk handkerchief has disappeared.

You then invite a member of the audience to step forward and open the matchbox . . . . and to remove the silk handkerchief from the box.

Those of you who have some knowledge of conjuring will recognize here a great improvement on an old trick. In its old form the box of matches was " faked," the matches could not be removed in full view of the audience (being, in fact, simply a false row of matches glued upon the bottom of the drawer) and the box could not be handled by the spectators . . . which is a point of considerable importance when one performs, as amateurs do, to small parties of one's intimate friends.

We will describe here an excellent trick with a borrowed handkerchief, a modern, abbreviated, version of an old trick called

THE INDESTRUCTIBLE HANDKERCHIEF

in which you appear to burn a hole in the centre of a borrowed handkerchief and to magically mend it again. To perform the trick you will need the thumb tip which you have already used in " The Bill in the Egg " and " The Smoke Trick," and a little piece cut from an old handkerchief, a circular piece a little more than three inches in diameter will do well. You tuck this little piece into the thumb tip in such a way that it may easily be withdrawn centre first, and you put the thumb tip in a convenient pocket until it is needed. In the same pocket you put a little box of snuff.

When the time comes, you put your right thumb into the tip and withdraw it from the pocket. You borrow a handkerchief (we advise you to use a man's handkerchief as ladies' ones are often so fragile) and you throw the handkerchief over your left forefinger so as to find the centre of it. You grasp the centre of the handkerchief with the right thumb and forefinger and remove the left hand from it, so that the handkerchief hangs corners downward. Now the left hand encircles the centre of the handkerchief and the right hand releases it, leaving the handkerchief hanging from the left fist. The right hand goes to the fist and pretends to pull out a little of the handkerchief Really it leaves the thumb tip in the fist and pulls up the little piece of cloth, which appears to be the centre of the handkerchief.

While this is being done you ask someone for a match (or you may take a lighted match from your pocket) and you remark about " a fact that few people seem to know; that handkerchiefs nowadays are made from a sort of fire-proof material." You hold the lighted match to the " handkerchief " as you continue: " They don't burn." As the piece of material catches fire you blow out the match and say; " Good gracious! This one does!" You blow out the flames and extinguish the glowing embers with finger and thumb, tucking the little piece back into the thumb tip and withdrawing the latter upon your thumb. You roll the handkerchief into a loose bundle with its centre inside it and put it down upon the table. Then you take the snuff box from your pocket and leave the thumb tip behind. Opening the box, you sprinkle a little snuff upon the handkerchief and, after a pause and a muttered incantation, you shake out the handkerchief and show it completely restored.

We have deliberately left to the end of our Handbook the famous trick which we mentioned at the beginning, the world's oldest conjuring trick

THE CUPS AND BALLS

Which is performed with three metal goblets or cups and a number of small balls. It is a trick which, at the moment, is rather neglected in this country, but it is a trick which every amateur should learn to do, if only because it pro-vides such excellent training in those two great virtues of the sleight-of-hand performer, Timing and Simulation. As, in addition, it is a trick which gives excellent scope for acting you will understand that its acquisition is a veritable education in conjuring. In France it enjoys great popularity and no French performer would deem himself worthy of the name of " prestidigitateur " if he could not perform " le Jeu des Gobelets." It is the principal stock in trade of the Egyptian " gilly gilly " men who astonish the tourists in the land of the Nile. A celebrated Iranian performer, long resident in Paris, Medjid Kan Rezvani, has made known to European conjurers the version of the trick favoured by the " magicians " of his native land, which uses large metal or china bowls and little bundles of cloth in place of balls. Akin to this version is the one performed by the itinerant conjurers of India, who use little wooden bowl-shaped cups each with a foot by which they are always handled. Still farther east the Japanese conjurers revert to the shape of the European cups of goblet type, but make them out of thin wood and paper instead of metal. Which brings us back home to certain English conjurers who use plastic beakers, paper picnic cups, or old ice-cream containers. These seeming practicalities add nothing to the effect and we advise the reader to purchase a proper set of cups worthy of the dignity of this classic of legerdemain.

But, to learn the trick, the reader can use with advantage three ordinary tumblers whose transparency will permit him always to see what is transpiring, and for balls he may use rolled up pieces of paper. Later he will be able to select his cups and balls with some knowledge of what he is purchasing.

Our predecessors in conjuring appear to have used nutmegs for balls and the French conjurers still call their balls " muscades." It is possible that oak apples were also used. Little cork balls were later introduced and are still largely employed, but balls of sponge rubber (cut from rubber bath sponges) were " discovered " twenty or thirty years ago, and are very popular, since they are extremely easy to use. Nearly all versions of the trick finish with the production beneath the cups of a number of large balls, or other objects of convenient size, such as apples, oranges, onions, tomatoes, small clockwork toys, live birds . . . the list is limited only by the ingenuity of conjurers, which seems to be without limit.

The sleights with the cups and balls are many and we shall only give you a selection of the simplest and the best.

Later, when the trick has taken your fancy, as we know it will, you can read some of the many different books and articles written about the trick during the last four hundred years, and increase your knowledge.

First you must learn to conceal one of the small balls in your hand. The " classic method " is to " palm " it by gripping it at the root of the second and third fingers, as shown in Fig. 21. To get the ball into that position you

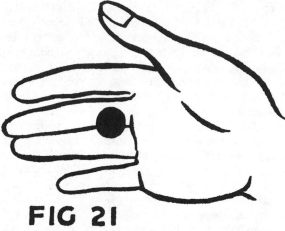

FIG 21

pick it up between first finger and thumb and roll it across the fingers with the thumb, which holds it in position for a moment while the middle fingers open very slightly and then close again to grasp the ball. It is a method more suitable, in the Author's opinion, to fleshy hands than to thin and bony ones.

A second method is to hold the ball in the crook of the little finger as we explained in Part I and illustrated in Fig. 3. This method has been used by many celebrated performers but there is really little to choose between the two methods, each has its advantages and, perhaps, its disadvantages, and you may use both or either of them. Give each of them a good trial before making your decision.

The second thing to learn is to make a ball disappear

from your hand, and this we have taught you already. You simply simulate the action of putting the ball into the other hand and, as you do so, you roll it to the root of the fingers or the crook of the little finger and conceal it there. We would once more remind you of the need to follow with your eyes the supposed passage of the ball and to keep your gaze upon the hand that is supposed to hold it while that hand moves away. The hand that conceals the ball must be held quite naturally and, if possible, used in some other action. After a moment the ball is commanded to disappear and the closed hand is slowly opened to show that the command has been obeyed. Do not imagine that it is a matter of great dexterity or of " clever sleight-of-hand." It is simply a matter of Simulation, Timing, and, above all, of Acting.

The third thing to learn is to secretly introduce a ball beneath a cup. This is quite simply done by lifting a cup, with a ball concealed in the hand, and dropping the ball on to the table, beneath the cup, at the exact moment when the cup is replaced. This action you have already learnt in the trick of " The Surprising Tumbler " in Part I.

The fourth thing to learn is to apparently place a ball under a cup while actually keeping it palmed. One of the most effective methods is to first pretend to put the ball into the left hand while really palming it in the right. The right hand then tilts one of the cups as it stands upon the table, the left hand pretends to slip the ball beneath, and the right hand allows the cup to fall back into position.

Finally you should learn a little movement with the cups which the French conjurers call " the gallop " because, when it is done rapidly, it produces a noise like hurrying hoofs. A set of cups is so made that when they are standing one upon the other there is room for a ball, or two balls, between them. This is depicted in the sectional illustration, Fig. 22. Pick up the stack of cups by grasping the lowest one with the left hand. Grasp the uppermost cup with the right hand. With a very slight upward swing of the hands, take the top cup from the stack and place

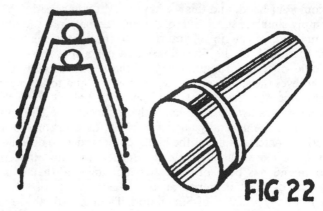

FIG 22

it mouth down upon the table. The ball within the cup, because of the little upward swing, remains within it and is carried away inside it. Repeat this movement, placing the second cup upon the first, with its ball carried within it because of the momentum of the little upward swing, and then place the third cup upon the second. Thus the stack of cups has been reversed, and the balls which were at first beneath the top and middle cups are now beneath the bottom and middle ones. To the spectators it appears that you have merely reversed the order of the cups and they are quite unaware of the balls within the stack. Practise this movement until you can do it with the minimum amount of upward swing and take care that it is indeed a little swing and not a jerk, which would attract suspicion.

From these elements many different routines may be constructed when we reveal the additional " secret " that, while the performer appears to use only three balls he actually uses *four*, apart from the large balls produced at the end of the trick. If you read the old books on conjuring you will find some astonishingly long routines with the cups. We do not advise you to copy them for you are unlikely to find a modern audience who would be prepared to sit through such a tedious exhibition. It is better for your routine to be too short than too long, to leave the spectators asking for more, than wishing you had not done quite so much, and we will give you a routine of model brevity.

Commence with your three large balls (or your potatoes, tomatoes, or other objects) and three of your small balls in your left coat pocket. The three cups are nested together with the fourth small ball within the outer one.

Begin by displaying the cups and, with an action similar to that used in the " gallop " arrange them in a row upon your table, secretly leaving the hidden ball beneath the left hand cup. Take one of the small balls from your pocket and pretend to place it under the right hand cup, but really palm it in the right hand. Command the ball to pass from cup to cup and make a suitable gesture over them, *with the right hand, the hand that palms the ball*. Then, simultaneously, lift the two cups with both hands and show that the ball has passed. Replace the cups on the table leaving the extra ball under the right hand cup.

Pick up the ball that is on the table, apparently place it in the left hand (really palming it in the right) and offer to pass it under whichever cup the audience may select. If the right hand cup is chosen you simply vanish the ball and lift the cup to show that it has arrived, but if one of the other cups is chosen you first lift that cup and place it aside from the others, introducing the palmed ball beneath it as you do so, then you vanish the ball from your hand and apparently pass it under the selected cup. In either case the palmed ball is left beneath the chosen cup as the latter is replaced upon the table.

A second cup is dropped on top of the one that conceals the extra ball and the visible ball is put on top of it. The third cup is taken in the right hand and crashed down upon the other two. The three cups are immediately lifted all together to reveal the ball lying on the table. The effect is as though the ball was knocked right through the cups.

The " gallop " move is then made, stacking the cups again, and the " knock through " procedure repeated, after which the cups are ranged in line, with the galloping action, the extra ball being left under the right hand cup.

A second small ball is now taken from the left coat pocket and the two balls are passed, one by one, underneath the right hand cup. To do this you pretend to put one of the balls into the left hand but really palm it in the right hand. You vanish this ball and lift the cup to show the extra ball which was already beneath it. In replacing the cup over the ball you introduce the palmed one. You now vanish the second ball in the same way, and show two balls beneath the cup. You put the cup down on one side and leave the extra palmed ball beneath it.

The tempo of the trick should now be speeded up, lest it become tedious. Although to the expert there is a great deal of difference between the various passes that are possible with the cups, to the audience they are all very similar, simply small balls passing from cup to cup and place to place.

Put the two visible balls on top of the left and middle cups and take the third ball from the pocket. Apparently put this ball into the left hand but really palm it in the right, and vanish it with a throwing movement towards the right hand cup. Grasp the middle cup and, without lifting it from the table, tilt it rather violently so as to toss the ball that rests upon it into the left hand, which you hold beside it in readiness. As the cup returns to rest release the palmed ball so that it falls beneath the cup. Vanish the visible ball with a tossing movement towards the middle cup. Repeat the tilting movement with the third cup and vanish the third ball in its turn with a throwing movement towards that cup. Now lift the cups one by one, showing a ball under each one, and replace them over the balls. You will still have the fourth ball palmed in the right hand.

Say: " Some people think I use more than three balls. They are right. Let us count them." Lift the right hand cup, displaying the ball beneath it, which you count as " one," and replace the cup on the table beside the ball, leaving the palmed ball beneath the cup. Pick up the visible ball with the right hand, pretend to put it into the left hand but really palm it in the right, and apparently drop it into your left hand coat pocket. Repeat all these movements with the second cup, counting " two," loading the palmed ball into the cup and pretending to drop the visible ball into your pocket. Do the same with the third cup, counting " three " but this time really put the small ball into the pocket and bring out, finger-palmed, in the left hand, one of the large balls.

Now lift the right hand cup, showing another small ball, counting " four," and transfer the cup to the left hand, thus, automatically but secretly, introducing the large ball into the cup. Put the cup down with the large ball beneath it, put the small ball into your pocket, and bring out the second large ball in the finger palm. Lift the second cup, showing the small ball beneath it, which you count as " five," transfer the cup to the left hand, placing it right over the large ball, put the cup down with the large ball beneath it, pick up the small ball and put it into your pocket, finger-palming the third large ball in exactly the same way as before. Load this large ball into the third cup in exactly the same way, and drop the " sixth" ball into your pocket. Then with a crescendo of " Seven, *eight*, NINE " tip over the cups to show the three large balls.

Although it should at this stage be unnecessary to do so we will, nevertheless, remind you of the need to diligently practice all the movements and then to rehearse the whole routine before attempting to show it even to your friends. Do not be in a hurry to show it to them, learning the trick is very good fun, and it is almost impossible to give it too much practice.

We regret that the time has come for us to leave you, although we could have continued on this fascinating subject for many more pages. We hope to meet you again in our companion Handbook of Card Conjuring.

Reading this book will have made you realize that conjuring is something more than mere quickness of the hand and that a knowledge of " how it is done " is not sufficient; you must also know *how to do it*. Let us recapitulate and bring together the general ideas you have gathered in the course of our Handbook.

First you should always remember that a conjurer is an *entertainer*, that conjuring is a branch of *acting*. While you are performing you will do your best to convince your audience that you are a person endowed with marvellous powers. When you have finished performing you will drop all pretence and admit that all is make belief. That is not to say that you will tell people how you produce your mysteries . . . Heaven forbid! But you will freely admit that all is illusion and if, as sometimes happens, people refuse to accept your disclaimer and insist on crediting you with supernatural powers, it is no business of yours, you are not bound to try to convince them. As long as you do not foster their credulity you may rest with an easy mind.

Remember next that in sleight-of-hand *timing* is more important than quickness, *deftness* more valuable than dexterity. Remember also that a natural action will always pass without comment while an unnatural action will immediately draw the attention, and the suspicions of the audience.

Try to imagine, especially when you first practice a trick, that you really do the things that you pretend to do. You will be able then to produce a better imitation of a real magician, which is the object of conjuring.

Practice the details of all your tricks very thoroughly and when you can do all the necessary movements with the utmost ease rehearse the whole trick as one entity, talking and behaving as though you were appearing before an audience, even to the extent of bowing to acknowledge the imaginary applause! Do this, not once, but many times, until you know your trick thoroughly, from beginning to end, and can do it almost without thinking. Then arrange your tricks in sequence to make a programme and rehearse this programme as a whole (making sure that the requirements of one trick do not clash with those of another) and then finding out how long it takes to present your " act."

Since beginners invariably go on far too long we would mention that *a very fine conjurer* may safely present a performance of thirty minutes' duration in a drawing room, of fifteen minutes on a concert platform, and of ten minutes on the vaudeville stage. All others should keep well within those limits.

Remember also, that when you are performing upon a platform or stage you should keep there. Do not continually run down amongst your audience to have things inspected or handled. If you need members of the audience to assist you, get them to come up upon the stage and seat them comfortably there. Thus the people at the back of the hall will be able to see what is going on as well as those in the first three rows.

Were we to leave you at this stage you might with justice ask " Where do we go from here." So we will tell you a little about the world of conjuring.

You are aware, of course, that your conjuring education has not been completed by the study of this Handbook. You still have much to learn. First you might add to your repertoire a selection of card tricks taken from the Handbook of Card Conjuring. And, as your skill and experience increase, you should certainly attempt some of the classic feats of conjuring such as the Linking Rings, the Billiard Ball Trick, and others which we have not dealt with in this volume as they are at present beyond your skill.

There is a very well-organized conjuring world having its own papers, its own books, and its own clubs and societies. America does not lack for organized magical societies. There is the time-honored Society of American Magicians with its nationwide local Assemblies, and monthly publication, " M.U.M." The International Brotherhood of Magicians, with headquarters in Kenton, Ohio, embraces many local " Rings " and publishes an important monthly periodical, " The Linking Ring." A Magicians Guild has a large professional membership, and other worthy individuals seriously devoted to magic; the monthly Guild organ is " Genii, The Conjuror's Magazine." An independent magazine for magicians published quarterly in New York City is " The Sphinx," which has just celebrated its fiftieth year of publication. Numerous other magical societies and clubs scattered throughout the United States play an eloquent role as part of the " grass roots " of magic, some catering to different age groups, sexes, collectors, and other common interests.

You will find the conjuring world an excellent one, famous for its good fellowship and containing men of all ranks and races, creeds, colours, and occupations. There is one general qualification for entrance . . . . a love of good conjuring.

BIBLIOGRAPHY

SELECTED AND ADVANCED WORKS

Annemann, T. *Practical Mental Effects*. (J. J. Crimmins, Jr., *ed.*). Max Holden, New York City, 1944.

Dhotel, J. *Magic With Small Apparatus*. Fleming Book Co., York, Pa., 1947.

Gaultier, C. *Magic Without Apparatus*. Fleming Book Co., York, Pa., 1945.

Hillard, J. N. *Greater Magic*. C. W. Jones, Minneapolis, Minn., 1938.

Tarbell, H. *Tarbell Course in Magic*. Vols. I-V. L. Tannen, New York City, 1927-1948.

Young, M. N. *Hobby Magic*. Trilon Press, Div. of Magazine & Periodical Pntg. & Pub. Co., Inc., Brooklyn, N. Y., 1950.

INDEX

97

CARD TRICKS

By
Wilfrid Jonson

Edited by Chesley V. Barnes

Dover Publications, Inc., New York

CONTENTS

CONTENTS—*continued*

PREFACE

THE scope of this book is very similar to that of its companion volume *A Handbook of Conjuring* and, while an acquaintance with that work is not essential, its perusal is recommended, since, although the technique of conjuring with cards is very different from that of ordinary conjuring, the principles of its presentation remain the same. This Handbook, like its companion, aims at illustrating those principles with a representtive selection of tricks which the amateur can perform without an excessive amount of practice, and will not require the reader to spend weary hours in the pursuit of excessive dexterity.

We would impress upon the reader the plain fact that the first aim of the conjurer is to entertain. If he will always remember that fact he will not go far wrong. For our part we shall refrain from including in this handbook any tricks which, however mystifying they may be, are boring, such as those in which the pack is four times dealt into thirteen heaps, and similar rigmaroles sometimes dear to compilers of books on card conjuring.

While pure dexterity with cards can, in the hands of a master, produce astonishing results, the majority of card tricks are effected by subtlety and misdirection more than by skill. The tricks themselves are often very simple and the art of the conjurer lies in dressing them up so that they appear to be miraculous. The beginner usually pays too little attention to this part of his business : neglects the dressing and spoils the trick. We shall clothe each trick in an appropriate costume and ask you to notice the skill with which the costume conceals the trick's weak points ; how the dressing distracts the spectator's mind from the fallacy which he must not be allowed to perceive.

LONDON, 1950   WILFRID JONSON

PART 1

*" Why he does what he likes with the cards,—when he's got 'em,
There's always an Ace or a King at the bottom "*

THE Author of the Ingoldsby Legends was neither the first
nor the last gentleman of the cloth to betray an astonishing
knowledge of card conjuring. To have " an Ace or a King at
the bottom " or, indeed to have any *known* card there, is a
great advantage to a card conjurer, as our first trick will show.

" THAT'S IT "

With a card that you know upon the bottom of the pack,
you put it down upon the table and ask a spectator to cut it
into two parts. Invite him to take a card from either portion
and to show it to the company, without letting you see what
card it is. When the card has been shown to all, ask the
chooser to replace it upon either portion and note carefully
upon which heap he does replace it, but do not let your
interest in this point be apparent to the spectators.

If he replaces the card upon the portion that was previously
the uppermost part of the pack, tell him to drop the other
portion on top of it. Let him then cut the pack and complete
the cut in card playing fashion.

But should he replace the card upon the other packet, the
original bottom part of the pack, ask him to cut that portion
and complete the cut, thus burying the selected card in that
packet, to put the two halves of the pack together and to cut
once more.

Perhaps we had better clarify this business of cutting for
the benefit of any readers unacquainted with card playing
practice. In games of cards the person who shuffles the pack
places it upon the table before a second player who cuts by
lifting off a portion of the cards and putting them down on the
table by the side of the remainder of the pack. The dealer
then *completes the cut* by picking up the original lower portion

9

and placing it upon the other. So, when these actions are combined by one person, to *cut and complete the cut* one lifts off a portion of the pack and puts it down on the table. One then picks up the remainder of the cards and puts them on top of the other portion. Cutting the pack is often regarded as the great safeguard of the honest player against the crooked gambler, and many card players display a faith in the virtues of cutting which is not borne out by the facts, as will presently be clear to you.

But to return to our trick. Whichever of the two procedures outlined above has been followed, the practical result is the same, the original bottom card of the pack has been placed immediately above the selected card.

You now take the pack and turning it face upwards, spread it from left to right in a long overlapping row, so that the indices of all the cards can easily be seen. With a little practice you will find that, with a good clean pack of cards, you can do this with one swift and skilful sweep of the hand. Now you hold your forefinger an inch or two above the cards and say to the chooser of the card : " I will pass my finger slowly along the cards like this. When it passes above your card I want you to think to yourself 'That's it.' Do not say anything, do not move a muscle, but every time my finger passes over your card simply think to yourself, ' That's it.' "

You pass your finger slowly along the row of cards from one end to the other and you look for the card you know, the original bottom one. The chosen card is the one below it, the one to its right in the row of cards. You do not pause when you reach it but carry on to the end of the row and say : " I did not get it that time. Again please." You carry your finger back along the row and a little way past the selected card ; then you pause and let your hand, with its pointing finger, swing in pendulum fashion, above the section of the row of cards in which the selected one lies. Then in a hesitant fashion you lower your finger and let it fall upon the chosen card.

In card conjuring one can often do more by intelligent planning and anticipation than by much sleight-of-hand and it would be a great pity if, at the conclusion of the preceding trick, one failed to take advantage of the fact that the cards are all spread out before you. So, before you gather them up you will remember the third and fourth cards from the bottom, that is from the right hand end of the overlapping row. Then you slip one finger beneath the top card, the card at the left hand end, and neatly gather up the overlapping row of the cards with one quick sweep of the hand. Much of the charm of good conjuring lies in the precision and dexterity with which the performer handles the cards and even such a simple action as gathering up the spread out pack can be done with elegance and distinction.

A MATHEMATICAL CERTAINTY

Knowing the names of the third and fourth cards from the bottom you put the pack down upon the table and ask one of the spectators to cut it into two heaps. When he has done so you ask him to touch one of the heaps. And here we come to an artifice often used in conjuring . . . . to apparently give a spectator a free choice when, in reality, whatever he may say the trick will take the same, premeditated, course. If the spectator touches the original bottom half of the pack you ask him to pick up that half, while you yourself pick up the other half. But if he touches the original top half you pick that up yourself, saying, " Very good. Will you take the other half then." Notice that you do not ask him to *choose* one of the heaps but simply ask him to *touch* one of them.

You now ask the spectator to " do everything that I do. Will you count your cards first." You count by dealing the cards one by one on to the table. The spectator does the same and as counting in this manner reverses the order of the cards, the two cards that you know were previously the third and fourth from the bottom will now be the third and fourth from the top of his heap of cards. Announce the number of cards in your heap and ask how many he has. Behave as if the matter was important. Actually it has nothing whatever to do with the trick but it is valuable " misdirection." Whatever number he announces ask him to discard one card. He will naturally discard the top one.

Ask him next to continue doing exactly as you do. Take the top card of your heap and slip it into the centre. Wait while he does the same. Take a card from the bottom and put it into the centre. Take a second card from the top and place it in your right coat pocket. Take another from the bottom and put it in the centre of the cards you hold. Take one more card from the top and put it into your left coat pocket. Put your cards down on the table. If the assisting spectator follows all these actions, which have been deliberately designed to drag so many red herrings across the trail, the card in his right-hand coat pocket is the one that was originally the third from the bottom of the pack and the card in his left-hand coat pocket is that which was originally fourth from the bottom.

You bring the trick to a climax by saying, " It is a mathematical certainty that this card in my left-hand pocket being the . . . ." (you bring it out and name it as you show it) " the card in your right-hand pocket is the . . . ." (you name the first of the two cards you have remembered) " and this one being the . . . . " (you take the card from your right-hand pocket and name it also) "the one in your other pocket is the . . . " (You name the second card you have remembered.) " Am I right, sir ? "

FALSE SHUFFLING I

If it is useful to know the card on the bottom of the pack, it is still more useful to be able to shuffle the cards and yet keep it there. It is not a difficult thing to do, in fact it is quite the simplest form of False Shuffle. But first we had better make sure that you know how to shuffle a pack of cards, for many people do not.

A good shuffle is one that mixes the cards thoroughly and leaves them so that neither the shuffler nor any spectator knows even the approximate position of a single card. We will confess at once that a really good shuffle is very rarely made but we will tell you how you may make a fairly good one. Take the pack in your left hand, face downwards, its left edge resting on the palm of your hand, the bottom card lying against your fingers and your thumb lying upon the top card of the pack. Grasp the pack by its ends with the right hand, the fingers at the far end of the pack and the thumb at the near end, and lift up all but a few of the top cards, which you retain in the left hand by a slight pressure of the left thumb. As the right hand raises the bulk of the pack the cards remaining in the left hand fall face down upon the left fingers. The right hand returns with the balance of the pack and a few more cards are deposited upon those in the left hand, being half dropped and half pulled off by the left thumb. The process is repeated until the whole of the pack has been returned to the left hand in little instalments. That is the true shuffle.

Let us ask you to remember two technical terms which will facilitate future description, for conjuring also has its technical jargon. The action of drawing away the underpart of the pack is called an " under-cut." The action of shuffling the cards in the right hand on to those in the left is called " shuffling off."

To false shuffle without disturbing the bottom card you first undercut three quarters or more of the pack but, as you do so, your left finger tips press against the face of the bottom card and keep it in position so that it remains in the left hand beneath the top cards. The balance of the pack is then shuffled off and the bottom card will have remained unchanged.

THE SEVEN HEAPS.

Having secretly noted the bottom card of the pack you false shuffle the cards to leave the bottom one undisturbed and put the pack, face down, upon the table. You ask a spectator to divide the pack into seven heaps, and you remember the position of the heap with your noted card at the bottom. Such a known card, by the way, is called a " key card " and we shall thus refer to it in the future.

You ask the spectator to remove any card from any of the seven heaps, to remember it, to show it to the other spectators, and then to drop it on the top of any heap.   That done you gather the heaps together again, apparently haphazardly, but actually you take care to drop the heap with the key card on top of the chosen card, and to leave the chosen card somewhere near the centre of the reassembled pack. You should handle the heaps neatly and carelessly ; neatly so that you may not be suspected of any sleight-of-hand, carelessly so that the fact that you keep track of the position of the card will not be observed. Pick up each heap by its ends between the second finger and the thumb and drop each one daintily upon the next. Ask the spectator now to cut the pack and to complete the cut, and observe the depth of his cut. If he cuts deep, that is to say, if he lifts up more than half the cards, the selected card will be left somewhere near the bottom of the pack, while if he cuts high the card will be towards the top.

Take the pack and, holding it face upwards, casually spread the cards between your hands. Look for the original bottom card (the key card) and quickly notice the name of the card below it, to the right of the key card in the face up pack. This is the selected card and since you know its approximate position in the pack, you should need only a quick glance at the cards to find it. Close the pack and shuffle it casually. Let us suppose the chosen card is the six of spades. Take any club and any red card from the pack and place them face up upon the table. Ask the spectator to fix his mind very strongly upon the colour of his card. Pause for a moment and then, since the selected card is a spade, pick up the red card and put it back in the pack and take a spade from the pack and put it down beside the club. Ask the spectator to think then of the suit of his card. After a moment's hesitation return th club to the pack. Turn the pack face downwards and begin deal cards very slowly on to the table, counting aloud and saying

" Ace, two, three, four, five, six .... You are thinking of the six of Spades. Is that right ? "

Notice the dressing please. To the spectators the trick will appear less like a card trick than like an experiment in thought reading.

FALSE SHUFFLING II

It is sometimes more useful to know the top card than the bottom one and when that is so the simplest method, very often, is to secretly glance at the bottom card and then to shuffle it to the top. This is very easily done by undercutting about three quarters of the pack and shuffling off until only a few cards remain in the right hand. The cards are held in the right hand between the thumb and the second finger, and you will find it a simple matter, at this point, to slightly straighten finger and thumb so as to hold only the bottom card and let all the others fall on to the pack. The last card is then dropped on top.

We hope that you are trying all these things as you come to them. You will make no progress in card conjuring by reading this book and sitting back and thinking about it. You must take the cards in your hands and try the actions as we describe them. Although we shall not ask you to learn anything very difficult even the simplest piece of conjuring technique requires a certain amount of practice.

We hardly think it should be necessary for us to explain how one may shuffle the top card of the pack to the bottom, but for the sake of completeness we will describe the simple procedure.

Commence the shuffle by drawing off the top card with the left thumb and then shuffle off the remainder of the pack. It is as well to immediately shuffle the pack again, keeping the card in its place on the bottom.

You should notice that by combining these two shuffles you may take the top card of the pack to the bottom at the same time that you shuffle the bottom one to the top.

THE CHANGING CARD

Secretly notice the bottom card of the pack, shuffle it to the top and hand the pack to one of the spectators. Ask him to think of a number. Tell him he may choose any number he wishes but that, to save time, you would suggest a number under twenty. When he has decided upon his number, turn your back and ask him to deal on to the table the number of cards he thought of; quietly, so that you will not be able to hear the cards fall. Ask him then to turn up the top card of those in his hand, to remember it and to show it to the other spectators, to replace it, to replace the cards he dealt, to cut the pack, and to complete the cut.

When he has done all this (the effect of which is to place your key card above his chosen card) you take the pack from him and holding it so that the spectators cannot see the faces of the cards, you spread it in a fan and find the key card. The one to the right of it will be the selected one. Let us suppose the selected card is the eight of Clubs. Draw the next card to the right, which we will suppose is the two of Hearts, over the eight of Clubs so as to conceal it and spread the cards a little so that the two cards, lined up as one, are a little free from the rest of the fanned pack. Hold the fan in the left hand and lower it so that the faces may now be seen by the spectators. Grasp the two cards between the right hand first finger and thumb and say : " Your card was not the two of Hearts, was it?" (naming the visible card). Raise the fan again so that the backs of the cards are towards the spectators and, as you do so, draw out the rear card of the two, the selected eight of Clubs and place it face down on the table. To the spectators it will appear that you have put the two of Hearts upon the table. Cut the pack to leave the two on the top.

Spread the pack in a fan again and remove another card *in exactly the same way as you did the first*, that is, show it in the fan, name it, and remove it as you turn the back of the fan to the spectators. Put this card, which we will suppose is he four of Diamonds, on the table beside the first.

Ask the assisting spectator to touch " one of the cards, the two of Hearts or the four of Diamonds." If he touches the four, turn it over and return it to the pack, then ask him to put his hand upon the other card and hold it tightly. If he touches the eight of Clubs, however, the supposed two of Hearts, tell him to keep his finger firmly upon it, turn up the four of Diamonds and return it to the centre of the pack. The " choice " is forced and in either case the spectator keeps his hand upon the chosen card while he believes he has the two of Hearts.

Ask the name of the selected card and say you will make it change places with the two. Ruffle the pack, that is to say, holding it in the left hand with the thumb across its back, lift up the ends of the cards with the right second finger tip and then release them so that they make a rustling, crackling noise. Then turn over the top card of the pack . . . .the two of Hearts !

Ask the spectator to turn up the card beneath his hand . . . . it is the selected one !

FALSE SHUFFLING III

We shall now ask you to learn a kind of false shuffling which is rather more complicated but which you should be able to acquire without difficulty thanks to your practising of the simpler kinds. We will call it the Pick Up Shuffle. It can be used for a variety of purposes but we will describe it first as it is used to retain a number of cards undisturbed upon the top of the pack, in other words a false shuffle to retain the top stock.

Commence the shuffle by under-cutting the pack, as we have already described, leaving the top cards which you desire to retain (the top stock) and a few more in the left hand. The bulk of the pack, in the right hand, should be held solely by the second finger and thumb, leaving the other fingers, and particularly the third one free. Bring the right hand down to the left so that the cards it holds cover the top stock and, beneath them, grasp the top stock with the right third finger against the right thumb. Leave a good packet of cards in the left hand and lift the right, carrying the top stock away hidden beneath the rest of the cards. Shuffle these cards off until the stock is reached and then drop that on top.

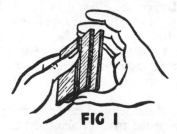

FIG 1

Figure 1 shows the position as the right hand moves upwards carrying away the top stock concealed beneath the other cards. The stock is held between the third finger and the thumb, and the other cards are held by the second finger and the thumb. The illustration, of course, shows the position as you see it yourself. The hands should be held so that the spectators see only the backs of the cards.

The shuffle is not difficult to do but you must practise it until you can do it practically without thinking about it and can pick up the top stock beneath the other cards without the slightest hesitation.

THE SENSE OF TOUCH

It is very convenient to give every trick a name by which it may be remembered, but the fabrication of titles is not always easy.

To be able to shuffle a pack and leave certain cards undisturbed on the top is of little value without a way of finding out what those cards are, or of secretly putting certain known cards in place. Many books on conjuring blithely ignore this difficulty and leave the beginner to solve the problem by himself. He sometimes solves it, as we have seen an amateur do, by using a different pack for every trick, each one having been arranged beforehand ! We shall teach you a trick now which **will give you the opportunity to find a few cards and to put** them on the top of the pack. The cards we shall seek are an ace, a two, a four, and an eight, all of different suits, which we shall need for the following trick. To prepare for one trick in the course of another is a very useful stratagem. The trick we give you will also teach you another method of using the known card upon the bottom of the pack.

Begin by glancing at the bottom card and remembering it ; then shuffle the pack without disturbing that card. Spread the pack between your hands, in a wide fan, as neatly as possible, and ask a spectator to choose one. When he has drawn a card, ask him to show it to the rest of the audience without letting you see it. Unless there is some good reason to the contrary it is always wise to have this done. Without this precaution you are at the mercy of a single person, who may forget the card he drew or even maliciously deny it. While the card is being shown close the pack, cut it and complete the cut, bringing your key card, your known card, to the centre, but hold a little division in the pack by inserting the tip of your little finger beneath the key card as shown in Figure 2. Such a division in the pack is called a " break ".

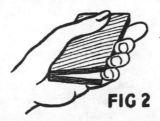

FIG 2

You now ask the selector to replace his card in the pack and you cut the cards and hold out the bottom half towards him. He replaces his card upon it and you drop the other half of the pack on top. But you have cut, of course, at the break held by your little finger tip, and so, the selected card is beneath your key card. You now shuffle the pack, taking care not to separate the two cards, by drawing off a fairly large packet of cards when you approach the middle of the pack where the two cards lie.

You now state that you have a very remarkable sense of touch, sensitive to even the slightest vibrations of thought. You ask the selector of the card to keep his mind upon its identity while you deal the cards upon the table.

You push the top card half way off the pack with your left thumb and run your right fingers over its face as though you were feeling its pips. You turn the card so that all may see it and then deal it face down upon the table. Without seeming to do so you glance at the face of the card yourself. A little experimenting will show you just how much the cards must be turned for you to be able to see the faces without the fact being obvious to the spectators. You continue dealing the cards one by one like this, quickly feeling the face of each one and throwing them haphazardly down on the table, and you watch for your key card. You also watch for the four cards you require, an Ace, a two, a four, and an eight of different suits, and as you come to these you deal them a little to one side so that presently you will be able to gather them up separately from the rest of the pack.

You should have found your four cards by the time the key card appears. You know that the next card is the selected one and you must not pause when you reach it but show it and deal it face down like the others. However, you carefully notice exactly where the selected card falls and you mark it by dealing another card on to its back. You deal a few more cards and then you suddenly stop as you feel the face of the next one. With a smile of satisfaction on your face you say to the spectators : " My remarkable sense of touch tells me that the next card to turn up is the selected one." Then you stop, as if bewildered by the expressions of incredulity shown by the spectators, all of whom have already seen the selected card dealt on to the table. You finger the card on top of those that remain and repeat : " Yes, the next card I turn up will be yours." The way in which this is received will depend a good deal upon the manners and breeding of your audience and upon the degree of intimacy between you, but people have been found rash enough at times to bet that the next card is not the selected one. In which case you repeat your statement : " The next card I turn up will be yours " and *turn up the selected card on the table.*

During the ensuing laughter you gather up the cards, quietly putting your Ace, two, four, and eight on the top of the pack, *in that order.*

THE MATCHING CARDS

With your Ace, two, four, and eight upon the top of your pack you execute the Pick Up Shuffle to leave them undisturbed and, placing the pack upon the table, you ask a spectator to cut it into two portions. When he has done so you pick up the original top half and invite him to take the other. You ask him to shuffle his cards and you do the same with yours. Actually you false shuffle yours by first shuffling off four cards, one by one, and then shuffling the rest on top of them. This is a very convincing form of false shuffle but its only result is to transfer your four top cards to the bottom of your half pack.

You now place your cards in your right coat pocket and invite the spectator to do the same with his, and you announce a further demonstraton of your remarkable sense of touch. For once you may tell your audience what you are going to do before you have done it, although, as we explained in the Handbook of Conjuring this is not, as a general rule, a wise thing to do. You state that you will ask the assisting spectator to draw a card from his pocket, haphazard, and by sense of touch alone you will draw cards that match it from your pocket. And this you do.

Let us suppose that your four cards, which are now on the *bottom* of the half pack in your pocket, are the Ace of Clubs, two of Diamonds, four of Hearts, and eight of Spades. The spectator draws from his pocket the ten of Clubs. You draw from your pocket the bottom card, the Ace of Clubs, saying " This matches the suit." Then you withdraw the second card, the two, leave the third, and bring out the eight, saying : " And these two give the value." It is best not to look at the cards but to run the finger tips across their faces to sustain the fiction that the sense of touch is alone responsible.

As another example : if the assistant drew the Ace of Spades you would draw the first and fourth cards from the bottom of your half pack, an Ace and a Spade.

For the three of Hearts you would produce your Ace, your two, and your Heart.

Counting Jacks as eleven, Queens as twelve, and Kings as thirteen, all the cards in the pack can be matched by your Ace, two, four, and eight.

THE PICK UP CONTROL

The theme of a very large number of card tricks is that spectators draw cards from the pack, remember them, and replace them. The conjurer then finds the cards in some ingenious way.

To do this the conjurer has to control the selected card in some unsuspected manner so that while it appears to be lost in the pack it is really kept in a known position, generally on the top of the pack. The old books from which we learnt the business, so many years ago, had practically only one method of control, the Two Handed Pass, which is really a secret cut. It is an excellent method, and we use it ourselves, but, unfortunately, it is so difficult that several years of patient practising must be spent to acquire any mastery of it, and a life-time may be passed in a vain effort to perfect it. Fortunately other methods have been invented during the last fifty years, years which have seen a revolution in the technique of card conjuring, and one of the best of these methods uses the Pick Up Shuffle which we have just taught you.

You spread the cards between your hands in a wide open fan and invite a spectator to choose one. When he has shown it to the rest of the company you invite him to return it to the pack, which you begin to shuffle from the right hand into the left. You pause in your shuffle and extend your left hand towards him and, quite naturally, he replaces his card upon the others in that hand. Apparently you at once shuffle the rest of the pack on top of the chosen card but actually, when the right hand comes down with its packet, you pick up a few cards, including the selected one, beneath it, and carry them away with the cards in the right hand. You then complete the shuffle and leave the selected card on the top of the pack.

THE CARD AND THE NUMBER

One of the most effective ways of revealing a selected card which has been " lost " in the pack is to find it at a numerical position chosen by a member of the audience. We shall give you a simple and amusing method.

Let a spectator choose a card, show it to the company, and replace it as you shuffle the pack. Bring the card to the top of the pack by means of the Pick Up Shuffle and then tell the chooser of it that you will invest him with your powers for a moment and enable him to find his card himself. Ask one of the other spectators to give you a number and suggest a number under twenty to save time. Let us assume that twelve is chosen. Hand the pack to the selector and instruct him to hold it in his left hand, to snap his fingers above it, and to order his card to fly to the twelfth place in the pack. When he does this (he will generally be rather sheepish about it) shake your head and say " Oh no, not like that ! "

Take the pack from him saying, " You won't get any results like that. You were not concentrating." Quickly count off eleven cards, by dealing on to the table, and turn up the twelfth, asking if it is the selected one. It is not. Replace all the cards on top of the pack and the selected card, originally on top, will now be the twelfth from the top.

Hand the pack to the spectator and ask him to try again. Tell him he must concentrate upon the job and do it with confidence. Ask the second spectator what number he chose, as though you had forgotten it, and get the selector to name his card and order it to fly to the chosen position.

Let him count down for himself and find it.

THE CORNER CRIMP

He would be a rather poor and ill-equipped conjurer who always used the same method to control a selected card, and we will now introduce you to another method which is very simple but, if properly used, very effective. You simply bend the inner right hand corner of the bottom card of the pack and use that card as a key card. Such a bend in a card is called a *crimp*. The corner crimp is easily made by placing the first finger tip underneath the corner and pulling down with the second finger tip as shown in Figure 3. Of course

FIG 3

the right hand rests above the pack, its thumb at the inner end and its fingers at the far end, and hides the left hand while it makes the crimp. In the illustration we have shown the left hand alone to make the action quite clear. The crimp should not be made too strongly. There is no need to break the corner of the card and the more expert you become in its use the less you will need to bend the corner.

You may crimp your card either before you start your trick or while the chooser of the card is showing it to the other spectators, but in either case you then cut the pack to bring the crimped card to the centre. When you ask the chooser to replace his card you have the pack lying face down in your left hand and you lift up half the pack with your right. In doing so your right thumb finds the slight break in the pack made by the crimped card and cuts the pack at that point. The selector replaces his card and you drop the half pack fairly on top and deliberately square the cards.

You pause for a moment and make some remarks regarding your trick and then you cut the pack again, once more cutting at the crimped card and bringing the selected one to the top of the pack. Immediately you false shuffle the pack, first shuffling the selected card to the bottom and then shuffling it back to the top.

Practise cutting at a crimped card, in the manner we have described, until you can find it at once, without hesitation, by the sense of touch alone. You must not look at the cards when you do this.

THE REVERSED CARD

An excellent way of revealing the selected card after you have brought it to the top of the pack is to find it turned face upward, and this may be done readily in the following amusing fashion.

With the pack in the left hand in the position for dealing, and the selected card on top of it, you pull out the bottom card and, showing it, ask if it is the chosen one. As you show the card your left thumb pushes the top one a little way off the pack to the right and you slip the tip of your left little finger beneath at, so as to separate it slightly from the rest of the pack. You next drop the bottom card face up on top of the selected card on top of the pack and, still keeping the little finger beneath the chosen card, you close the other fingers around the two cards so as to square them perfectly together. Now with your right hand you grasp the two cards as though they were one, between the second finger at the far end and the thumb at the near end, and remove them from the pack.

The left thumb now pushes the new top card over to the right so that it overlaps the pack. The left hand edge of the two cards in the right hand (which are held as if they were one) is placed beneath the right hand edge of the top card, and the latter is tipped over to fall face up on the top of the pack as you ask, " Is this the card ? "

The card is then pushed a little to the right by the left thumb and picked up by the right fingers underneath the two cards that they hold, and the next card is turned face up in the same way.

When six or seven cards have been turned over, shown, and taken in the right hand in this way, you appear to lose patience, and say, " Oh well, I give it up. What was your card anyway ? " At the same time you turn all the cards in the right hand face down on top'of the pack, which will leave the selected card, face up, six or seven cards down in the pack.

On hearing the name of the selected card you say, " Oh, that card always was a nuisance. We will find it another way."

Cut the pack and then run your thumb rapidly across the edge of it to make a crisp crackling noise. This for effect. Then spread the pack in a long overlapping ribbon of cards so that the chosen one shows, face up, in the middle of the row of face down cards.

SENSITIVE FINGER TIPS

The principle of the corner crimp is used again in our next trick, which is presented as another demonstration of the conjurer's extraordinary sense of touch. The performer appears to succeed in finding, by sense of touch alone, a card which has been simply thought of by a spectator.

Commence by handing the pack to a spectator to shuffle. On receiving it back take the top five cards and, spreading them in a fan, ask the spectator simply to think of one of them. You glance at the cards yourself and remember their order. To do this it is not necessary to remember their complete names and it is far easier not to do so. For instance, I take the five cards from the top of the pack that lies beside me as I write, which happen to be the Queen of Diamonds, King of Spades, seven of Clubs, four of hearts, and five of Clubs, and I simply remember Queen, King, seven, four, and five. It is only necessary to remember suits when two or more cards of the same value appear amongst the five.

When the spectator has thought of a card you close the fan and secretly crimp the corner of the batch of five cards. Then you cut the pack, drop the five crimped cards on the bottom half, and replace the upper half above them. You then take the pack and shuffle it, when you will find that it is very easy to shuffle without separating the five, which will hang together in one batch because of their crimped corners. Finally you cut the cards, so as to bring the five crimped ones to the top of the pack, and you put the pack into the inside breast pocket of your coat, which it is wise to empty for the purpose of this trick.

You now " build up " your effect. That is to say, you enumerate the preceding stages of the trick to impress upon the spectators the remarkable nature of what is being done. A card has been selected by being simply thought of and has been thoroughly shuffled into the pack. Only one person knows the identity of the card. The pack is out of sight in your pocket and only your remarkable sense of touch can aid you to find the card.

Now you ask the spectator to name his card and, as soon as you hear its name you know its position. For example (using the cards we have already mentioned) you repeat to yourself Queen, King, seven, four, five and you know if the selected card is the first, second, third, fourth, or fifth from the top of the pack in your pocket. You put your hand into your pocket, count down to the required number, and slowly draw out the selected card.

THOUGHT DIVINED

We have previously called your attention to the excellent ruse of preparing for one trick while performing another, and we will now give you another example of its efficacy. At the close of the preceding trick the pack was in your inside coat pocket and, as you remove it you leave behind two cards in preparation for the present mystery, which links up well with the last.

You hand the pack to another spectator requesting him to shuffle it and then to hand you any three cards. You hold the cards in front of him in a fan and ask him to think of one of them. Once more you remember the order of the cards.

You now pretend to put the three cards into your inner coat pocket but actually, hidden by your coat, you thrust them into the upper right hand vest pocket and then let your finger tips enter the coat pocket. At this moment you open your coat a little so that the spectators may see the fingers leaving the coat pocket.

In the last trick you found a card that had been thought of, using only your sense of touch. In this one you are going to discover which of the three cards were thought of. You ask the spectator to fix his mind upon his card. You gaze at him earnestly as though you were endeavouring to read his mind and, after a moment, you put your hand into your coat pocket and remove one of the cards you left there at the start. You glance at it (without letting it be seen) nod to yourself as though you were satisfied, and replace it on the pack, saying, " I don't think you are thinking of that one."

You go through the same performance again, as convincingly as you can. First you read the man's mind, then you remove the second card from the coat pocket and return it to the pack, saying " And not that one either."

You continue : " And before I show you that I have succeeded would you mind naming the card you thought of." As soon as you hear its name you know if it is the first, second, or third card in your vest pocket. You keep your coat over the pocket as you quickly find the correct card and draw it out.

PALMING

The technique of card conjuring, as we have mentioned before, has been practically revolutionized during the last fifty years. The nineteenth century conjurer almost invariably controlled a selected card by using the Two Handed Pass, generally bringing it to the top of the pack. He would then palm the card, that is to say he would conceal it in his hand, and he would hand the pack to a spectator to be shuffled. When he received the cards back he would replace the palmed one on the top of the pack and proceed with his trick.

This procedure is excellent but, while it is still used at times by some of the experts, it has gone somewhat out of fashion. The general tendency today is for the conjurer to shuffle the cards himself, thus considerably speeding up the action of his trick.

But there are occasions when it greatly strengthens a trick to allow the spectators to shuffle the pack, and there are other tricks to which palming is essential, so we will give you a method. It would be possible to give you a hundred methods but not very useful to do so. Ever since card tricks and card games were invented the hunt had been on for an indetectible method of palming . . . . and the hunt is still on. We are always appreciative of efforts to extend the technique of conjuring but we feel that the existing methods of palming are quite adequate if the conjurer knows his real business, which is to conduct himself in such a manner that at the moment he is palming his card or his cards the attention of the spectators is diverted to something else. So we shall teach you a comparatively simple but excellent method of palming which you can use for either one or a number of cards. First examine Figure 4, which shows a card in the

FIG 4

palm of the hand. It stretches from the first joints of the fingers almost to the heel of the hand, which is slightly bent in a *natural* manner. The card bends to follow the curve of the hand. Notice now the position of the thumb, which is *relaxed*. A great fault of many amateurs is to stick the thumb

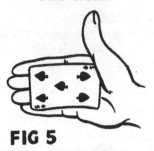

FIG 5

out stiffly, as in Figure 5, when they have palmed a card, and the unnatural appearance of the hand " telegraphs " the fact to all the spectators. Of course, when a card is palmed the back of the hand must always be kept towards the audience, but that, alone, is not sufficient. The hand must be held and *used* in a natural way, so that the presence of the card is not even suspected.

To palm the top card of the pack you proceed in this way. Hold the pack in the left hand in the position for dealing and, with the left thumb, push the top card about three-eighths of an inch to the right, so that it overlaps the side of the pack. Bring the right hand over the pack as if to grasp it by its ends, fingers at the far end and thumb at the near end. The tips of the first three fingers should rest against the far end of the pack so that the crease lines which show where the fingers bend will rest against the edge of the top card. As the little finger is shorter than the others its tip will now rest upon the far right hand corner of the top card. We hope you have a pack of cards in your hands as you read our description and can ascertain that the facts are as we have stated them. Press gently down with the right little finger upon the far right hand corner of the top card and, since it is overlapping the pack, it will be levered up into the palm of the hand. It will be necessary to raise the left thumb very slightly to let the card do this, and the less the thumb moves the more imperceptible will be your palming. As soon as the card strikes the inside of the right hand the hand contracts very slightly to secure it, and then grasps the pack and

FIG 6

moves away with it as shown in Figure 6. To the spectators it should appear that the pack was simply taken from the left hand into the right.

When it is required to palm a number of cards a little preliminary action is necessary. Let the right fingers and thumb rest naturally upon the ends of the pack while the left thumb counts off the number of cards it is desired to palm by pushing them off the pack a little way to the right. Square them up and leave them overlapping the pack about three-eighths of an inch. Now let the right hand leave the pack, to make some gesture or perform some action, and then bring it back to the pack to palm the batch of cards exactly as if it were only one.

The difficulty in learning to palm is mainly psychological. The beginner lacks confidence, thinks that the action is too obvious, holds his hands too tensely, feels self-conscious, and generally fumbles the job. You must practise the simple movement until you can do it almost unconsciously, remembering that the only source of confidence is reliance in your own ability.

We will now give you a few tricks to exercise your skill in this new acquisition.

HYPNOTISM !

You ask the company if they believe in the possibility of mass hypnotism and assure them that, at times, the thing is possible. You will try an experiment ! Very solemnly you make " hypnotic passes " towards them and you then request that one of them select a card from the pack and show it to

the others. You have the card replaced in the pack and you
bring it secretly to the top, either by using the Pick Up Control
or by means of the Corner Crimp and a simple cut. Then you
palm the selected card from the top as you take the pack in
your right hand, and you tell your audience your story.

"A card has been selected," you say, "while you were all
under hypnotic influence." You return the pack to the left
hand and spread it in a fan, all the while keeping the selected
card palmed, and you continue, "As a matter of fact, it was
this card." You remove a card from the fan and show it to
the company as in Figure 7, which shows your own view.
Observe how you boldly use the hand which palms the card,

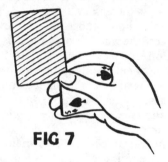

FIG 7

so boldly that none will ever suspect its presence ! You
continue, "Undoubtedly all of you being under hypnotic
influence believe that the card you saw was some other one.
What, by the way, was the card you thought was chosen ?"
On hearing its name you say, "Let me prove to you that you
never really saw that card by showing you that I put it into
my pocket before we started." Without haste you replace
the card you hold on the top of the pack and thrust your hand,
with the palmed card into your pocket and withdraw it,
holding the selected card !

We commenced the last sentence with the words "without
haste." Please read it again because those two words are
most important. Beginners are generally in too much hurry
when they have a card palmed. It seems to burn the flesh and

make them anxious to be rid of it. Remember that, in conjuring, quick movements always attract attention and, perhaps
because of the old untruth " the quickness of the hand de-
ceives the eye," quick movements are always suspected.

You must carefully practise this action of pretending to
take the card from your pocket. You must particularly watch
to see that when the hand moves to the pocket its back always
remains towards the audience so that they have not the
slightest glimpse of the card. Once the hand is safely within
the pocket the card is released from the palm and retaken at
the finger tips.

THE CARD IN THE POCKET

This is a trick which has enjoyed considerable popularity
amongst conjurers and is very puzzling to the spectators.
You first hand the pack to one of the company to shuffle and
then you ask him to think of a number. You suggest that he
should think of a number under twenty in order to save time.
You now turn your back upon him and instruct him to quietly
count down in the pack and remember the card that lies at the
number of his choice, and to replace the cards counted. You
tell him to count very quietly so that you will not be able to
hear the cards fall and you ask him to tell you when he has
finished his task. Then you turn and take the pack from him.
You hold it behind you for a moment while you appear to be
deep in thought. You then remove a card from near the bottom
of the pack and bring it forward, its back to the spectators so
that none can see what card it is, and you pretend to put it
into your pocket. Actually, as soon as the hand is in the
pocket, you palm the card and bring it out again. You immediately take the pack in the hand that is palming the card
and, as you place the pack on the table in front of the assisting
spectator you add the card to the top of the pack.

Now you build up your effect by pointing out how remarkable it would be if, without any clue and without asking a
single question, you had succeeded in finding a card, chosen

B

by merely thinking of a number, and had placed that card in your pocket.

You pick up the pack and ask the assisting spectator to tell you, for the first time, the number he thought of. Let us suppose he says " Fourteen." You deal thirteen cards down on to the table, slowly and deliberately, and place the fourteenth in front of him, saying, " This should be the card you remembered, the fourteenth. What card was it ? " When he has named it you ask him to turn up the card in front of him and he finds, of course, that it is a different one, because you have added one card to the top of the pack. The card he remembered is now on the top of the pack. As he turns up the card on the table and everyone is watching him, you quietly palm the top card of the pack. Then you calmly put your hand into your pocket and withdraw it holding the palmed card at the finger-tips : and another miracle has been accomplished.

THINK OF A NUMBER

We are reminded of another excellent trick in which a spectator counts down to his chosen number, as in the last, but the general effect is quite different.

First secretly crimp the bottom card of the pack, as we have already taught you, and then shuffle it to the top. Hand the pack to a spectator and ask him to think of a number. Again suggest a number under twenty, to save time. When he has made his mental choice turn your back and tell him to deal that number of cards noiselessly on to the table. When he tells you he has done that, tell him to show the card that remains on top of the pack to the rest of the company, to replace it, to replace the cards he has dealt, to cut the pack, and to complete the cut.

Turn and take the pack from him, remarking that the card having been selected and replaced under test conditions, all your powers will be required to find it. Actually, as you will have discovered if you have performed the actions yourself, the selected card lies beneath the one with the crimped corner.

Look at the end of the pack. The crimped card will show quite plainly to one who knows what he is looking for. Cut the pack so that the crimped card becomes the bottom one, and the selected card will be on top. False shuffle so as to leave the card there and then ask for its name.

Slide the top card, the chosen one, to the right so that it overlaps the pack about an inch. Immediately grasp the pack with the right hand, by its ends, and slap it down upon the table. The pressure of the air against the overlapping card will cause it to turn over and appear, face up, upon the top of the pack.

This last effect is a very old way of revealing a selected card and is generally called " The Revolution." A little experiment will be necessary before the effect becomes quite certain. The pack should be tossed on to the table from a distance of about eighteen inches, and not too violently. But it is not sufficient to " let fall the pack " as a famous author has said when describing the trick.

EDUCATED FINGERS

Still using the principles we have taught you already, we give you now a beautiful trick which combines some classic card technique with modern simplified methods. The effect, as the audience see it, is that two cards are chosen and replaced in the pack, which is then shuffled by a spectator. The pack is then put into the performer's pocket and the two cards are found by his educated fingers.

You begin by letting two people each draw a card from the pack, and while they are showing their cards to the rest of the company you crimp the corner of the bottom card and cut the pack to bring the bottom card to the centre. Then you cut the pack at the crimped corner and have the first selected card replaced, dropping the cut back on top of it. You repeat this with the second card and then cut at the crimp once more to bring both cards to the top of the pack. Next you palm the two cards from the pack and hand it to a spectator to shuffle thoroughly.

With your right hand, which holds the two palmed cards, pull out the lining of your trousers pocket and show it empty. Replace the pocket and leave the two cards within it. Leave the cards standing on their ends. Take the pack from the shuffler and put it into the pocket also. Leave the pack on its *side*. Thus the two cards already in the pocket will not become mixed with the pack.

Ask the name of the first selected card. Put your hand into your pocket and pretend to feel for the card in the pack. After a moment or two bring out the card you require. Remember that if you had the cards replaced in the order in which they were taken the first selected card will be the second card in your pocket.

Produce the other card in the same way.

There we have what Professor Hoffmann called " the bare bones " of the trick—the first essentials, the foundations upon which one has to build. We will now examine our procedure in more detail.

When cutting at the crimp for the selected cards to be returned try to make your cut as late as possible. That is to say do not cut the pack long before the spectator is ready to return his card. He may become suspicious and try to return it to another part of the pack. The pack should rest naturally in the left hand. You ask the selector of the card if he will replace it and you extend the left hand towards him. As he holds out his card you cut the pack, using only the second finger and thumb of the right hand. The thumb finds the crimp almost automatically and the cut is made without hesitation at the correct spot. The selector replaces his card upon the lower portion and you *drop* the upper portion on top of it, letting it fall four or five inches, to land with an audible " smack ". This emphasises the apparent fairness of the procedure and makes the subsequent discovery of the card all the more remarkable.

The next point to watch is the palming of the two cards after they have been brought to the top of the pack. It is best done as you move towards the person you ask to shuffle the pack. It is a simple matter to push the two cards a little to the right in readiness for the palm. Speak directly to a member of the audience seated on your left and ask him if he will shuffle the pack. As you move towards him palm the cards in your right hand and take the pack in the same hand, holding it by its ends, and give him the pack. Your own inclination would be to give him the pack with the other hand, the empty one, but this would be quite wrong. Give him the pack with the right hand and hold the left so that he can see it is empty and he will not dream that you are withholding any cards.

Your technical troubles are now nearly over. But you must be careful how you hold your hand as you pull out and replace the lining of your trouser pocket. Try this over, half a dozen times, in front of your wardrobe mirror.

When you receive the pack from the shuffler hold it at the tips of the fingers and let all the audience see that you place it deliberately and fairly into the pocket. But do not make any remarks about this. It is always a mistake to say " Observe that my hands are empty . . . . notice that I do not do anything tricky " . . . and so on. Such remarks only remind the audience of the possibility of trickery and spoil the enjoyment of good conjuring. And we hope your conjuring will be good.

Finally, when you are producing the cards from the pocket try to act as if you were really finding them in the shuffled pack . . . . finding two particular cards amongst fifty-two. And we think that you will find that your acting will be more convincing if you appear to be just a little bit astonished at your own success.

FALSE SHUFFLING IV

When the top stock is rather large, that is to say when you desire to keep in place on the top of the pack a fairly large number of cards, the Top Stock Pick Up Shuffle is not the best method to use, in fact seven or eight cards is the most that should be retained by that means.

To keep a *large* stock undisturbed, take the pack in the left hand in the usual shuffling position and undercut beneath the number of cards you wish to retain. Bring the right hand down to shuffle off and, with the left thumb, draw off the first card of the right hand packet so that it overlaps the left hand packet (the top stock) about three-eighths of an inch at the end nearer yourself. Then shuffle off the remaining cards. The pack will now be in the left hand with the top stock at the bottom separated from the rest of the pack by one card which protrudes at the near end, as depicted in Figure 8. Cut the

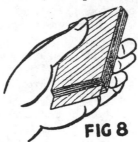

FIG 8

pack by picking up with the right hand the protruding card and all those above it. Complete the cut and your top stock will once more be in place.

A card left protruding from the pack in this manner is called, in the jargon of the craft, a " jogged " card. It is " in-jogged " when it protrudes from the near end of the pack and " out-jogged " when it protrudes from the far end. A false shuffle using this principle is a " jog shuffle " and the simple one we have just taught you is the Top Stock Jog Shuffle. Some very marvellous things may be done by shuffles based on this principle . . . . but that is another story.

SPELL IT OUT

We shall now return for a while to the idea of knowing the card which is on the bottom of the pack and using it for a key card. We shall acquaint you with some variations of that idea in this and the succeeding sections.

To discover a selected card by spelling its name has been, for long, a favourite effect with conjurers. As you spell the name of the card, you deal one card for each letter, and the selected card is reached with the last letter of its name.

One of the simplest methods for achieving this effect is very similar to the one which we have already described for finding a card at a chosen number. (See " The Card and the Number.") You bring the chosen card to the top of the pack, which you hand to the chooser. You tell him to spell out the name of his card and to deal one card for each letter. He is to turn up the last card. Of course, the card he turns up is not the chosen one, and you blame him for not doing the trick properly. You replace the cards and show him how he should have done it. You deal one card for each letter of the name and turn up the selected card as you pronounce the last letter. The first attempt has put the card into the correct position.

The weakness of this method is that it can only be used once before the same people. After that they would be rather suspicious regarding the preliminary failure. We will give you another method.

If you examine the question of the number of letters required to spell the different cards of the pack you will find that all, except the Joker, may be spelt with eight, nine, ten, eleven, twelve, or thirteen letters when spelt in full as, for example, " Ace of Spades ", and that even the Joker can be spelt with thirteen if you call him " The Jolly Joker." Here is the table :

Ace, two, six, and ten of Clubs . . . . . eight letters

Ace, two, six, and ten of Hearts and Spades,
four, five, nine, Jack, and King of Clubs . . . . . nine letters.

Three, seven, eight, and Queen of Clubs,
four, five, nine, Jack and King of Hearts and Spades . . . . .
ten letters.

Ace, two, six, and ten of Diamonds,
three, seven, eight, and Queen of Hearts and Spades . . . . .
eleven letters.

Four, five, nine, Jack and King of Diamonds . . . . .twelve
letters.

Three, seven, eight, and Queen of Diamonds . . . . . thirteen
letters.

Or perhaps you will find this a more convenient form :—

Clubs .... five letters
Hearts and Spades .... six letters
Diamonds .... eight letters
Ace, two, six, and ten ....three letters
Four, five, nine, Jack, and King ..... four letters
Three, seven, eight, and Queen ......five letters.

Armed with this information you are able to perform the spelling trick in a different way.

Begin by spreading the cards between your hands and asking a spectator to select one. As you spread the cards, by pushing them to the right with your left thumb, you count them and separate the first twelve from the others. When the selector has made his choice you close the pack and hold a break under the twelfth card with the tip of your left little finger. After the selector has shown his card to the company you cut the pack at the break and ask him to return his card. You drop the cut on top of his card, square up the pack very deliberately, and make your Top Stock Jog Shuffle. The chosen card will then be the thirteenth from the top of the pack. To the minds of the spectators it is hopelessly lost in the pack.

You tell your audience that you have a most intelligent and well-educated pack. The cards even know how to spell their own names. You enquire the name of the selected card. If it is either the three, seven, eight, or Queen of Diamonds (or even the Joker) you simply run your fingers across the edge of the pack to make a sharp crackling noise, purely for " effect ", and hand the cards to the selector, telling him to deal one card for each letter of the name of the one he selected.

Should the card be any of the others you must calculate how many cards you must remove from the top of the pack to produce your effect. You do this by showing the selector how you wish him to count the cards by dealing them on to the table one by one so that everyone may follow. If the card is spelt with eight letters (ace, two, six, and ten of Clubs) you deal five cards in explanation. You pick up these cards and put them back *on the bottom of the pack*. Then you hand the pack to the selector for him to spell his card. For a nine letter card you would deal four, for a ten letter card three, and so on.

There are some people to whom all calculations are abhorrent and for whom the task of deducting four from thirteen is too difficult. There are others who find it impossible to remember the values of the cards and to work out the numbers of their letters, or at least, to do so quickly. We must confess that we have never liked work of this sort, either of memory or of calculation, when in the presence of an audience. When the Author is giving a conjuring show he wishes to be free to give the whole of his mind to the things he says and the way in which he says them, and he does not wish to be worried with either calculation or recollection. If you are like him you may prefer the following method, which makes use once more of the principle of the key card.

Invite a spectator to choose a card and, while he is showing it to the company, glance at the bottom card of the pack, remember it, and cut the cards so as to bring this key card to the centre of the pack, keeping a break below it with the tip of the little finger. Cut the pack at the break, let the card be replaced, drop the cut back on top, and square up the pack. The selected card is now beneath your key card.

Make a quick movement of the hands and run your thumb across the edge of the pack so as to make a rustling noise and arouse the suspicions of the audience. Stop, and say : "I beg your pardon. I hope you do not think I have done anything to your card. Let me show you it is still in the pack." Turn the pack face upwards and pass the cards from your left hand to your right hand one by one, showing their faces. Watch for your key card, the original bottom one. The one beneath it, the one to the right in the face up pack, is the selected card. Beginning with the key card, spell the name of the selected card to yourself as you pass the cards one by one from left to right. Omit the final " S " of the name of the suit, and when you come to the penultimate letter, look at the spectator and say : " Have you seen your card ? " and, as he replies to you, cut the pack to bring the last card you reached to the top. Now make the Top Stop Jog Shuffle and hand the pack to the selector for him to spell his card.

There is an extension of this idea which, we think, considerably improves it. You proceed exactly as above but when you run through the pack to show the cards you first spell to yourself, as you count, the name of the selected card, then you note the name of the card you reach when you arrive at the final " S ", and then you spell that card also, omitting the " S ". Let us suppose this final card is the king of Hearts. You cut the pack and you tell the spectator who chose the card that you are going to give him the power to find his card by spelling its name. First you will show him how to do it. " For instance," you say, " if I want to find the King of Hearts I concentrate my mind upon that card and flip the pack, so. Then I deal one card for each letter of its name, so . . . .

K - I - N - G - O - F - H - E - A - R - T - S

and the King turns up." You deal the King face up as you pronounce the letter S.

Now you hand the pack to the spectator and make him concentrate his mind upon his card and spell and find it for himself.

THE MARKED CARD

This principle of the Key card has many variations, such as that of the Marked Card, to which we now introduce you. You will often notice, when you are doing card tricks with a pack that has been used for games, a card with a definite mark upon its back, a cracked corner, or a spot of some sort. If you do not notice such a card you can always manufacture one by pressing your thumbnail into the corner of a card.

With your marked card, found by chance or made to order, on the bottom of the pack, you proceed exactly as we have already taught you. You have a card selected, you cut to take your key card to the centre of the pack, and you have the selected card replaced beneath the key. You can now shuffle the pack if you take care not to shuffle the centre portion, so that the selected card will remain beneath the key card.

An excellent way of proceeding then is to put the shuffled pack on the table and ask the selector to cut it into six or seven small packets. When he has done this ask him if he can tell in which of the packets his card lies. Undoubtedly he will say that he has no idea. Ask him to choose one of the packets. Spread the packet he chooses into an overlapping row and run the tips of your fingers along it, while you half close your eyes and behave as if this slight contact of the finger tips were conveying some information to you. Meanwhile you are looking for the marked card and as soon as you have ascertained that it is not within the packet you tell the selector that his card is not there, and ask him to choose another packet. Proceed in this way until you find the packet with the marked card and then announce the presence of the selected one.

Keeping track of the selected card, which you know is the one beneath the marked one, you spread the cards haphazardly over the table, using both hands. You take the spectator by the wrist and ask him to concentrate his mind upon the identity of his card. You steer his hand in a circular movement over the cards and then gradually decrease the size of the circle until it diminishes to a point directly above the selected card. You suddenly put the spectator's hand upon his card and let him turn it up.

You can imagine how strong the effect is, and often the spectator will examine the card, vainly seeking a clue to the mystery.

FROM THE FAN

We now come to another variation of the principle of the key card, one which is quite different from any that have gone before.

You hand the pack to a member of the audience to be shuffled, and, when you receive it back, you take the top ten or twelve cards and put the rest of the pack on the table. As you do so you glance at and remember the bottom card of your packet of ten or twelve.

Now you mix your packet of cards together in a casual way, using both hands, and you so contrive that at the end of the mixing your noted card will be the top card of the packet. You should not have any real difficulty in doing this. Now you spread the packet of cards into a very wide fan, so that all the cards are well separated from each other, and holding the fan in one hand, you invite a spectator to lift up one card by its corner, to peep at its index, and to remember its name. As the spectator does this you count and remember the number of cards between your key card, on top of the fan, and the card which the spectator peeps at.

You then close the fan of cards and, cutting the pack, bury the packet of ten or twelve within. Finally you cut the pack several times, each time completing the cut.

The position now is that the key card is lost somewhere in the pack and that the selected card follows it, separated by a certain number of cards which you know. You have only to find the key card to be able to find the selected one also.

It would be interesting to leave you to devise your own continuation to the trick but as we should be unable to enjoy the results, or even know if you arrived at any, we had better, perhaps, provide you with a conclusion.

If when you replaced the packet within the pack, you put it somewhere near the centre, and if, when you cut the pack, you did so an even number of times, the selected card and the key will be still somewhere towards the centre of the pack. Verify that please, while we wait a moment . . . . . Then if you cut the pack into three portions you may be fairly sure that the selected card and the key card will be in that portion which was the centre of the pack ? Good !

Cut the pack into three portions then and ask the selector if he has any notion as to which of the heaps contains his card. When he replies in the negative suggest that the centre heap be tried. Say : " I will just show you the cards in this heap. After I have shown you all the cards, but not before, tell me if your card is in this heap." Now you deal the cards into a face up pile and you count them as you deal. Let us suppose that there were six cards between the key and the selected card. As you deal, and count, your key card turns up, say, at the sixth card, you count on six more, and the next, the thirteenth, is the selected card. You remember its name, and you complete the dealing.

You ask the spectator if his card is in the heap, and when he replies in the affirmative, you turn the cards face downwards and hand them to him. You turn your back and hold your hands behind you and you ask the spectator to deal the cards on to your hands, one by one. As you feel the cards being dealt on to your hands you count them and, after the twelfth has arrived and before the thirteenth, you suddenly cry : "Stop ! You are holding your card ! Am I right ? "

You pause for a moment to permit the spectators to applaud if they wish to, as they should, and then you continue : " Now let me see if I can discover the name of your card. Put the card into your pocket so that I cannot see it, will you ? " When he has done that turn to face him and say : " I want you to think of the identity of that card and I will try to divine it." (Let us suppose for the sake of our description that the card is the three of Spades.) " First, let us see, is the card red or black ? It is black I think. Yes, I see from your eyes that it is black. A Club or a Spade, that is the question ? I will take a chance and say it is a Spade. It is. Now it might be a court card or a pip card. King, Queen, Jack . . . . no, I see it is a pip card. The ace ? No. The two ? No. The Three ? Yes ! It's the three. Am I right ? Thank you ! "

In some such fashion and with some such words, which will be much more effective than simply blurting out its name, you divine the card. If you act your part well, a good proportion of your spectators will half believe that you can read the man's mind, and will be willing and *pleased to believe it*. It is this that we meant when we said in our Preface that the art of the conjurer lies in dressing up his tricks. And when those tricks are well dressed up the spectators will find pleasure in believing in the reality of magic even though the belief only lasts while the performance continues.

THE SPECTATOR DOES IT

The variations of this theme of the discovery of the chosen card are almost as many as the variations which there are in the use of this principle of the key card. In the trick which we shall now give you the selector of the card appears to find it for himself.

First you have a card selected and, while it is being shown to the company, you turn your back so that you cannot see what card it is. While your back is turned you quietly turn the bottom card of the pack face upwards, cut to bring it to the centre, and hold a break beneath it with the tip of your little finger. You now turn back to the audience and have the card replaced, cutting at the break so that it is replaced beneath the reversed card, and dropping the cut back in the manner which should now be quite familiar to you. Your trick will be improved if you then give the cards a shuffle, taking care not to disturb the centre of the pack where the two cards lie.

In this, and in all tricks in which cards are secretly reversed in the pack, it is best to use cards the backs of which have plain white margins rather than the popular pictorial cards, now so much in vogue, upon which the colouring extends to the edge of the card. With these cards one must keep the pack very carefully squared up if the reversed one is not to be seen at the wrong moment, while with the white margin cards there is nothing to be feared even should the pack be slightly spread out.

But to return to our trick. You continue by asking the chooser to step forward and face the audience with you, and you tell him that you wish him to try a simple experiment with you, or rather, a not so simple experiment. You say to him : " I want you to hold the pack behind your back like this, and to do exactly as I tell you." In illustration you put the cards behind you, and you quickly turn the second card from the top face upwards. Then you hand the pack to the chooser and give him your instructions. " Hold the pack behind your back please. Keep it there all the while so that none can see exactly how this is done. Now take the top card and . . . . no ! better not use that one .. . . . put that on the bottom of the pack and take the next one. Now turn that card face up and thrust it into the pack, *anywhere you like.* Have you done that ? Good. Square up the pack please and then give it to me."

Now you turn to the audience and explain what has been done so that they may appreciate the truly marvellous nature of the effect. First a card was chosen at random and put back in the pack, which has been shuffled. The selector of the card has thrust a second card, face upwards, into the pack. And now comes the miracle. In some such words you make sure that the spectators really appreciate the worth of your trick. You must always do this. The conjurer who does not blow his own trumpet will find nobody else to do it for him.

You now take the pack and spread it in a fan until the reversed card can be seen. You are careful to do this slowly and deliberately so that all can see that you do not manipulate the cards in any way. You remove the reversed card and the card beneath it together, and you ask the name of the selected card. You slowly turn over the two cards you hold to show that the chooser has found his own card.

You can see, of course, what really happened. It is your original reversed bottom card which is next to the selected one. The card the chooser thrusts into the pack is the second one from the top which you had turned face upwards and which he turns face downwards, thus losing it in the pack.

TURN OVER

Here is another trick which bears some similarity to the last in that a card is found by another which is reversed.

The procedure is similar also. You have a card selected and you turn away while it is being shown to the company. While you turn your back you cut the pack to bring either a seven, an eight, a nine, or a ten to the bottom. You then turn this card over and count off the same number of cards as its value, reversing the order of these cards as you do so and finally replacing them on the bottom of the pack. That is to say, supposing that you bring an eight to the bottom of the pack, you first turn the eight face upwards, then you count off eight cards, taking the second on top of the first, the third on top of the second, and so on, and replace the eight cards on the bottom of the pack. The result is to leave the reversed eight, eight cards from the bottom of the pack.

Now you turn to the audience again and cut the pack, holding the break beneath the cut in the usual fashion. You have the selected card replaced beneath the cut and you have nothing more to do than to " work up " the effect.

You explain that you are going to ask one of the cards to turn over in the pack and that that card will enable you to find the selected one. You run your thumb across the edge of the cards and spread the pack in a fan until the reversed one appears. You cut the pack to make the reversed card the top one and call attention to the number of its pips, eight. You count down eight cards and ask the name of the selected one ; then you turn it over to show that another marvel has been produced.

THE FORECAST

Sometimes, instead of finding a selected card the conjurer forecasts the card that will be chosen and this, astonishingly enough, may also be done by the aid of our old friend, the bottom card of the pack.

You tell your audience that, after very many years of patient research, you have discovered a method of foretelling with comparative certainty the events that will occur in the immediate future. Unfortunately the events must occur within the very immediate future and your present time limit is within five minutes of your forecast. This limitation of time is extremely annoying and has kept you, up to now, from giving up work and making a real clean up on the football pools. However, it is rather interesting and you will give a demonstration of your ability with the pack of cards.

You take the pack and glance at the bottom card. You remember its name and you shuffle it to the top. Now, keeping the pack in your left hand, you take an envelope and a slip of paper and, using the pack to support the paper, you write on the latter, " The lady will cut the cards at the .... of .... " writing, of course, the name of the card you noted, now on the top of the pack. Of course, if you are performing amongst friends you would write the name of the lady you intend to ask to assist in this trick. The slip of paper you now seal in the envelope and, while you are doing this, you take the opportunity to push the top card a little over the side of the pack. Then, when you have pressed the flap of the envelope well down to seal it, which gives you an excuse to place the envelope on top of the pack again, you are able, very simply, to carry the card away beneath the envelope as you take the latter in your right hand. This card beneath the envelope is, of course, the one whose name is written upon the slip of paper within.

Now, with the pack resting upon the palm of the out-stretched left hand, you advance to the lady and ask her to cut the cards wherever she wishes. Impress upon her that she has perfect freedom to cut high or low, as she prefers. When she has cut the cards you say, " We will mark the cut with the envelope for a moment," and you put the envelope, with the card beneath it, on the bottom half of the pack, and ask the lady to replace the top half above the envelope. Then you hand the lady the pack, with the envelope sandwiched within it, asking her to hold them for a moment.

Now you recapitulate. A moment or two ago you wrote a forecast which you sealed in the envelope. The lady has now cut the pack at a point she freely chose, and nobody knows what card lies at that point. Could anyone have known beforehand ?

You ask the lady to lift up the envelope and to tell the company what card it is at which she has cut. When she has done that you ask her to open the envelope and read aloud your forecast ......

A CARD PUZZLE
We will conclude Part I of our handbook with an excellent puzzle with cards which is well worth showing if you will take

the trouble to learn it properly. It is done with the twelve court cards and aces and the object is to lay them out in four rows of four cards so that in none of the rows, horizontal or vertical, shall there be two cards of either the same value or the same suit. A possible arrangement is shown below :

Queen of Diamonds	Ace of Clubs	Jack of Hearts	King of Spades
Ace of Hearts	Queen of Spades	King of Diamonds	Jack of Clubs
Jack of Spades	King of Hearts	Queen of Clubs	Ace of Diamonds
King of Clubs	Jack of Diamonds	Ace of Spades	Queen of Hearts

All the explanations of this puzzle which we have seen tell you to begin by setting up the two diagonals with four cards of the same value, but this spoils the whole thing by making it appear too easy. Actually, even when the diagonals are set up, the thing is not so simple as it appears to be.

We are going to show you how to lay out the cards from left to right in four rows, explaining all the points it is necessary to remember in order to do so. We think the best way to do this will be for us to actually lay out the cards as we would if we were showing the puzzle to some friends. So we first take the court cards and aces from the pack and shuffle them thoroughly. Now we turn the cards face upwards and take the first one, which we put down on the table in what will be the top left hand corner of our square of cards. The card happens to be the Jack of Diamonds. The next card is the King of Clubs which we put down beside the Jack. The third card is the Jack of Clubs, which we pass by, since we have already both a Jack and a Club in the row and, in any case, the cards must be alternately red and black ones. The next card is the Ace of Hearts, which we put beside the King. Now a glance at these cards shows that to complete the row we require a Queen, and a second glance shows that it must be the Queen of Spades, so we find that card to make the first line . . . .

Jack of	King of	Ace of	Queen of
Diamonds	Clubs	Hearts	Spades

Now the second line must always commence with a card of the same value as the second card of the first line, but of the opposite colour. In the present case it must be a red king and, since the first vertical has already been started with the Jack of Diamonds we must use the King of Hearts. Now the two diagonals must consist of cards of the same value and the centre cards must be of the opposite colour to the corner ones. Our next card must therefore be a black jack, and as the King of Clubs heads the second vertical line we must put down the Jack of Spades. Our rule about the diagonal tells us that the next card must be a red queen and as the Queen of Hearts will not do we can only put down the Queen of Diamonds. An ace is needed to complete the line and must obviously be the Ace of Clubs. Our second line is completed then, and we have . . . .

Jack of	King of	Ace of	Queen of
Diamonds	Clubs	Hearts	Spades
King of	Jack of	Queen of	Ace of
Hearts	Spades	Diamonds	Clubs

The third line must always commence with a card of the same value as the third card of the first line. It must therefore be an ace and, as we have already two red cards in the first vertical line, we put down our remaining black ace, the Ace of Spades. Our next two cards will be determined by the rule of the diagonal and can only be the Queen of Hearts and the Jack of Clubs. The King of Diamonds must complete the line, giving us . . . .

Jack of	King of	Ace of	Queen of
Diamonds	Clubs	Hearts	Spades
King of	Jack of	Queen of	Ace of
Hearts	Spades	Diamonds	Clubs
Ace of	Queen of	Jack of	King of
Spades	Hearts	Clubs	Diamonds

It requires very little thought to see how one must arrange the last four cards to complete the magic square so . . . .

Jack of Diamonds	King of Clubs	Ace of Hearts	Queen of Spades
King of Hearts	Jack of Spades	Queen of Diamonds	Ace of Clubs
Ace of Spades	Queen of Hearts	Jack of Clubs	King of Diamonds
Queen of Clubs	Ace of Diamonds	King of Spades	Jack of Hearts

With a little practice you will become so expert at laying out the puzzle that you will be able to deal the cards almost without hesitation, while your friends will find it very difficult to do even though they start with the two diagonal lines.

PART II

WE will commence the second half of our Handbook with a simple piece of sleight-of-hand, of very great utility, which we shall ask you to learn before you go any further. You should find no difficulty in doing so. In this Handbook we do not ask you to learn anything that requires much dexterity. This piece of sleight-of-hand is called

THE GLIDE

and its object is to enable you apparently to deal the bottom card of the pack while in reality you slide that back a little and deal, in its place, the second card from the bottom.

It is done in this way. You hold the pack by its sides in the left hand, between the forefinger and the thumb, with the back of the top card facing the palm of the hand. You let the tips of the second and third fingers rest against the face of the bottom card, as in Figure 9. You turn the hand so that the

FIG 9

pack faces the ground and draw back the bottom card about half an inch, as shown in Figure 10, by a simple movement of the second and third fingers.

The right hand second and third finger tips now draw out the second card from the bottom, apparently the bottom one, and drop it on to the table. Then, by reversing the movement

FIG 10

of the fingers the drawn back card may be slid back to its former place.

The Glide may be used to change one card into another as, for example, to change an indifferent card into a selected one. You have a card selected and replaced in the pack and you bring it to the top by means of the corner crimp, for example. You now shuffle the pack by drawing off the top and bottom cards together and shuffling the rest of the pack on top of them, when the selected card will be the second from the bottom. Please try this shuffle before we go on. You will find that it is a combination of the shuffle to take the top card to the bottom and False Shuffle I which leaves the bottom card in place.

Now, holding the pack in position for the Glide, you show the bottom card to the spectators saying, " I suppose the shuffle has not, by any chance, left the selected card on the bottom of the pack ? " As the chooser replies you lower your hand, making the glide, and apparently draw out the card you have just shown and drop it on to the floor. But really it is the second card from the bottom, the selected one which you drop upon the floor. You ask the selector to put his foot upon it.

Now you ask for the name of the selected card and command it to change places with the card on the floor. You cut the pack to bury the card you have shown in the centre and you run your thumb sharply across the edge of the pack before asking the selector to turn up the card beneath his foot.

In the pages that follow we shall give you some further uses for this simple sleight.

THE INSEPARABLE ACES I

To avoid repeatedly having to ask the audience to select cards from the pack the practice has developed of performing tricks with the kings or the aces, which the conjurer removes from the pack himself. Of late years the aces have been most favoured since they are the most conspicuous cards in the pack. In the present trick you use the two red aces.

You run through the pack and pick out the two aces, which you throw down upon the table, and you secretly glance at the top card of the pack and remember its name. You then put the pack down beside the aces and ask one of the spectators, when you have turned your back, to first cut off a small packet of cards and put it upon the table to one side, then to take either of the aces and to place it on top of this small packet, next to cut off a further portion of the pack and to drop it on top of the ace, then to place the other ace upon the last portion, and finally to drop the rest of the pack on top and to square up the cards. You then ask the spectator to cut the pack twice, each time completing the cut.

You now turn round and, taking the pack, point out exactly what has been done. The two aces have been lost in the pack and separated from each other by an unknown number of cards. You hold the pack in the position for the glide and commence to deal the cards from the bottom, dealing them face up upon the table, as you remark that you will demonstrate that the aces are inseparable and, in spite of all, will be found together in the pack.

As you deal the cards from the bottom you watch for the original top card, which you have remembered, and as soon as it appears you know that the next card will be one of the aces. Instead of dealing this ace you make the glide, sliding the card back about half an inch. You must do this without the slightest hesitation or pause and you then continue to deal the cards until the second ace appears, when you at once deal the first ace upon it to show that the aces have come together again.

It will be interesting to ask if you now realize why we told

you at the beginning that you use the two red aces in this trick.
The point is that in the dénouement the aces are dealt in the
reverse order to which they were placed in the pack and if
you were to use the black aces this fact might possibly be
noticed by a wide awake spectator because of the conspicuous
nature of " old mossy face " the Ace of Spades.

THE INSEPARABLE ACES II

The effect is the same as in the last trick, the separated
aces come together again, but this time all the four aces are
used and all the action of the trick is done by the performer
without any assistance from the audience. This is a great
advantage in a card trick, and a welcome change from the
majority, in which the active participation of the audience is
generally required.

To lend a little verisimilitude to the story you will tell of the
inability to keep the aces separate it is as well to commence the
trick with them all together in the pack. As we pointed out
in Part I the best way to manage this would be to get the four
aces together in the course of a preceding trick, but another
way is to do so as you look through the pack for the Joker. You
fan the cards between your hands and hold a break when you
come to the first ace. You fan the cards further until you
come to the second ace. You draw this out of its position
and slide it back beside the first one. You do the same with
the third and fourth aces. You ignore the Joker if you come
to it before you have found all the aces, as you probably will,
and you return to it afterwards. Without comment you discard
the Joker. It is probably better to leave the audience wondering
why you did this than to give them an explanation that is not
entirely convincing.

Now you tell your story : that in a well-trained and properly
kept pack of cards the aces are always inseparable. Drag them
apart and, as soon as they can, they will fly together again.
You fan the pack, the faces of the cards towards the audience,
until you come to the aces, all together as you have stated,
and you draw them out and drop them upon the table.

Now, holding the pack in your left hand, spread into a wide fan, you push the aces half way into the fan in different parts of it, as shown in Figure 11. Apparently you do this

FIG II

haphazardly but really you take care to remember the name of the card to the right of each of the first three aces. The indices of all the cards being plainly visible when you fan the pack like this you will have no great difficulty but, to facilitate remembering the cards, it is as well to pick out three of the same suit. So, for example, you look along your fan and you see the seven of Hearts, behind which you put your first ace. You go farther along the fan until you come to another Heart, say the four, and you put the second ace behind that. You carry on until you come to, say, the King of Hearts, behind which you put the third ace, and all you need remember now is " seven, four and King of Hearts."

Next you close the fan, leaving the aces still half protruding from the pack so that the spectators can see quite plainly that they are separated from one another. Then holding the pack by its sides, you tap the ends of the aces and drive them slowly into the pack, which you then cut twice, each time completing the cut. You take care, also, to cut at about the centre of the pack each time, so that the two cuts practically neutralize each other and leave the cards as they were, although the spectators, with the trust which the public has in the efficacy of cutting, will not realize this fact.

You remark that although the aces have been well separated it will only take them a few moments to come together again and, holding the pack in the position for the glide, you begin to deal the cards, faces up, from the bottom of the pack. As you deal you watch for the first of your three memorized cards, in our example the seven of Hearts, and, as soon as it appears, you glide back the next card, which you know will be the first ace, and you go on dealing without a pause until you come to the second card which you have remembered.

When you were practising the Glide you probably discovered that an easier way to do the same thing was to push the bottom card back half an inch with the fingers of the right hand instead of pulling it back with the second and third fingers of the left hand. We hope you realized that this method, besides being less elegant, was less good and less undetectable as, always when it is used, there will be a slight hesitation before the card is dealt as the fingers push back the bottom card before drawing out the second one. However, it will be necessary to use that method now and to push back the second ace flush with the first with the right hand fingers, since the position of the first card prevents the use of the Glide. To cover the momentary hesitation before dealing, you deliberately pause, and say to the audience : " Surely we should have reached an ace by now ? "

Then you continue to deal the cards until you reach the third card which you have remembered, the King of Hearts in our example, when you pause once again and say : " Still no aces," as the right fingers push the third ace flush with the first two so that you may continue to deal indifferent cards.

You go on dealing until you actually come to the fourth ace when you say : " At last we have come to the ace, and the other three are with it " . . . . and you deal the three drawn back aces on to the first.

THE FOUR ACES I

Almost everybody has seen and nearly everybody knows the ancient trick with four kings which are shown, spread in a fan, with the three jacks concealed behind them. The fan is closed and the seven cards, apparently four, are dropped on the top of the pack. Now the first "king", really a jack, is taken from the top and slid into the pack a little way down. A second "king", another jack, is pushed into the pack half way down. A third is replaced in the pack three-quarters way down, and the last king, which may be shown, of course, is placed on the bottom of the pack. The pack is then cut and the four kings are discovered all together in the centre. While these childish manœvures are being carried out an infantile story of four burglars is told.

The trick in that form is so well-known that it is not worth doing, although it still appears from time to time in books on conjuring written by the ill-informed for the wholly ignorant. But the trick is the fore-runner of the modern Four Ace Trick, which is so popular that we have been unable to discover a conjurer who has never performed some version of it, and we have been informed that there are over a thousand different versions. In the method we shall describe for you we shall take advantage of the old trick being so well known to have a little fun with the audience.

This trick may well follow the last, in which case you will have the aces separate from the pack, but if it does not you will commence by running through the pack and picking out the four aces. And then you have your joke. You murmur an excuse and turn your back to the audience ! First you take the three top cards of the pack and slip them into your bottom left hand vest pocket, where they remain hidden by your coat. Then you arrange the four aces into a very trim fan which you hold in your right hand in a suspicious way, as if you were hiding something behind it. The pack you keep in your left hand.

Now you turn back to the audience and announce the famous mystery of the four aces.

If you are performing the trick before a small company of people in an ordinary room we suggest that you kneel down and do it all upon the carpet.

You put the pack down on the carpet and then, using both hands, you close the fan of cards rather clumsily and put them on the top of the pack, saying : " The four aces I place on the top of the pack, so." Then you pick up the pack and deal the aces one by one in a row upon the carpet saying : " Now I deal the aces in a row upon the floor." You pause for a moment and add : " Now everyone knows that the aces are in a row on the carpet." Again you pause. The peculiar action and the unnecessary statements will have made everyone dissatisfied that the aces are on the carpet as you say they are. Some expressions of doubt will surely be made. You raise your eyebrows and open your eyes in surprise . . . . and then you slowly turn over the four cards to show that they really are the aces.

Now you say : " Let's start again." You pick up the aces and place them on top of the pack. You say : " First I deal the aces in a row upon the carpet." You bring your right hand over the pack and grasp it by the ends while you run your thumb across the edge to make a suspicious rustling noise. Then you deal the four aces on to the carpet rather quickly and say : " Well, everyone knows that the aces are there this time."

Again the audience will dissent and after a pause, with an expression of mock amazement, you turn over the four cards to show the aces once more. As you do this you push the top three cards a little to the right of the pack with your left thumb and slip the tip of your little finger beneath them to hold a " break ". You say : " This is very strange. Let us start again."

You gather up the four aces and you drop them on the top of the pack. Then you pause as though a thought had just struck you and say : " I see what it is. You don't think I put the aces on top of the pack." Aided by the break held by the little finger you take the top seven cards in the right hand and put

the pack down upon the carpet. Now you take the seven cards
in your left hand, holding them at the finger tips as shown in

FIG 12

Figure 12. The thumb is on one side and the second and third
fingers upon the opposite side. The little finger rests against the
near end and the forefinger at the far end. Held thus the cards
are kept perfectly together so that it is impossible to see how
many there really are. You show that you have four aces.
You draw off the top ace, the little finger moving away to
permit this, and show it. You slide it back underneath the
packet as you say : " The first ace."

You do the same with the second and third aces, showing
them and putting them beneath the packet, but the fourth ace
you replace on top of the packet after you have shown it. As
a result of this manœuvre your packet of seven cards will be
arranged, from the top, an ace, three indifferent cards, the
other three aces.

Having shown the four aces you put them, very carefully
and deliberately, on the top of the pack and say : " Now, no
kidding this time," and you turn over the top card, an ace,
and turn it face down again.

Then you deliberately deal the four top cards on to the
carpet in a row from left to right and say : " Now on each ace
I deal three more cards." Commencing with the left hand
heap you do precisely what you say. As a result you will make
four heaps. The left hand heap will consist of the four aces.

The other three heaps will consist of indifferent cards. The audience should believe that each heap consists of an ace surmounted by three ordinary cards.

In the trick we called " A Mathematical Certainty " (Part I) we gave you an example of the equivocal choice, and here we give you another. Your object is to have the left hand heap, consisting of the aces, " chosen " by one of the audience. You say to one of the ladies : " Would you mind choosing from these heaps either the inner or the outer pair." If she replies " the inner " you pick up that pair and drop them upon the pack, but if she replies " the outer " you say " Good," and push those two heaps forward a little, using only one finger to do so. *Then* you pick up the two inner packets and drop them upon the pack. Then you say to the lady: " Right or left please ? " and whichever she chooses you pick up the heap that does *not* contain the aces and drop it upon the pack, interpreting "right" to mean your own right and "left" to mean the lady's left. You leave no time for consideration of the point but at once ask the nearest spectator to draw his or her chair a little nearer and place one foot upon the remaining heap.

Now you approach your climax. You may say : " You have probably heard that a remarkable affinity exists between the four aces, which cannot bear to be separated. In the pack here we have three of the aces. Beneath this gentleman's foot we have the fourth ace, selected by chance, with three ordinary cards. In a moment the three aces will fly from the pack to join the fourth beneath the gentleman's foot. There ! " You run your thumb over the edge of the pack and then spread the cards face upwards in a long row upon the carpet. " The aces have gone ", you say, " and the three ordinary cards that were under your foot have flown under my coat." Here you reach under your coat and pull out the three cards you put into your lower vest pocket at the beginning of the trick.

And you conclude by asking the man to lift his foot and to turn up the four aces !

THE GLIDE FORCE

For the first time in this Handbook we mention the word
" force " although the card " selected " in the trick called
" The Forecast " was actually a " forced " card. There are
various ways by which a conjurer may ensure that a certain
card, predetermined, is " selected ", although the person who
draws it deems that he has had a free choice. Then we say that
the conjurer has " forced " the card. Needless to say we speak
of this only amongst ourselves and never mention the word to
the public.

The method used by the experts is called the " Classic
Force " and we shall not describe it to you since it calls for
more skill than you can easily acquire, more than we have
undertaken to ask of you. For the moment we will show you
how you can force a card by means of the Glide, which is very
simple.

Put the card you desire to force upon the top of the pack
and then shuffle it to the bottom. (All forces are stronger if
they are preceded by a shuffle which gives the impression that
you have no knowledge of the position of any of the cards in
the pack.) Now hold the pack in the left hand in the position
for the glide, draw back the bottom card, and begin to deal the
cards slowly from the bottom, always dealing the second one,
of course. Ask someone to call " stop " at any moment. At
the request to stop, glide the bottom card back into position,
and then draw it half way off the pack and permit the person
who called to remove it, and place it in his pocket.

It is as simple as that !

THE FOUR ACES II

We shall now describe a trick with the four aces which is
of such great simplicity that you may hesitate, perhaps, to
believe that it really could be effective. But when your knowledge of conjuring has increased you will understand that it
is often the simplest tricks that are the most mystifying. The
simpler the solution the less likely it is that it will be considered.

We can remember, many years ago, seeing a well-known professional magician do this trick to a gathering of experts in the Magic Circle Club Room, and completely deceive all of them. And we can remember, also, their looks of blank astonishment when the simple secret was revealed to them.

The effect of the trick as it is remembered afterwards is that you shuffle a pack and place it upon the table. You ask someone to cut it into four approximately equal heaps. You turn over the cards on the top of the heaps and reveal the Four Aces.

The first thing to do is to get the four aces on the top of the pack and we will suggest a way in which you may do this without being suspected. First you glance at, and remember, the bottom card of the pack. Then you false shuffle to leave the card undisturbed, and you force it upon a spectator by means of the Glide Force which we have just described. You ask the spectator to put the card into his pocket without looking at it or letting anyone see what it is.

Now you ask the company if they think it is possible for you to discover the identity of the card that is missing from the pack by simply looking through it once only. The answer should be " No " because it is practically impossible to do this. You will have no difficulty, however, since you already know the card, having forced its selection. Let us suppose it was a six. Keeping the backs of the cards to the spectators you look through the pack and, every time you come to an ace you slip it to the top, while every time you come to a six you drop it, face down, upon the table. At the end you will have the four aces on the top of the pack and three sixes on the table. You turn the three sixes over and ask the spectator to remove the fourth one from his pocket. You gather up the four sixes and put them on the bottom of the pack.

Now you shuffle the pack, leaving the four aces undisturbed on the top, and put the cards down on the table. You ask a spectator to cut the pack into four approximately equal portions and, when he has done so, you look at them with a rather critical eye. It is impossible to give explicit instructions for the continuation of the trick because it depends so much upon how the cutting has been done, but you watch and note the position of the top portion of the pack which is capped by the four aces. We will call this heap A and the others B, C, and D. Perhaps C will be a little bigger than D. You say : " There are too many here " and you take two or three cards from C and put them on D. Then you seem to notice that B requires some cards and you take two (aces) from A and drop them on B. Then you take two more from A (aces again) and drop them on C. Then you observe that A is short and take a few cards from D to make it up. You also add a card from B (an ace). Then you take a few cards from C and put them on D, but decide that you have put too many and take one (an ace) back again. With that you appear to be satisfied.

You snap your fingers over the four heaps and then turn up the top cards, the Four Aces !

The movements we have given you are purely optional. You may use them if you wish or you may work out a series of movements for yourself, or you may improvise as the size of the heaps suggests to you. You have only to keep cool, take care to remember the position of the aces, and be careful not to overdo the thing and confuse yourself.

THE THIRTEEN PRINCIPLE

We stated above that it is practically impossible to discover the name of a card abstracted from the pack by merely looking through it once. We said " practically impossible " because we are not quite sure that it cannot be done by means of a mnemonic system and, in any case, we have seen so many fantastic things accomplished since we first dabbled in this conjuring business that we shall be reluctant always to use the word impossible without any qualification. But, it is not only possible but very simple to discover the card by going through the pack *twice*. Try it as you read our directions please.

Remove a card from your pack and place it aside, without looking at it please. Now go through the pack and add the " spot " values of the cards together, subtracting thirteen everytime your total exceeds that number, ignoring the Kings and counting the Queens as twelve spots and the Jacks as eleven spots. A simple example will show you that this is not so formidable a task as it may appear to be at first. I look through the pack that is beside my typewriter. The bottom card is the nine of Clubs, but I take no notice of the suits and simply think " nine." The next is the five of hearts. Nine and five are fourteen. I deduct thirteen and carry one. The next card is a seven which, added to one, makes eight. Another seven makes fifteen and again I deduct thirteen and carry two. The next card is a two (two and two are four) then comes a King, which I ignore, and a three (four and three are seven) followed by a Queen, which I count as twelve, taking my total to nineteen. I immediately deduct thirteen, reducing the total to six, to which I add the next card, a nine, making fifteen. I at once return to two by deducting thirteen, and I carry on in this way until I reach the end of the pack, when my final figure is eight. This is then subtracted from thirteen to give me the value of the missing card.

I look through the pack a second time for the fives and find the five of Clubs, five of Spades, and five of Diamonds, and I know that the abstracted card is the five of Hearts.

Do not think that you need to be a mathematical wizard to do this trick. It is very rarely that your figure goes over twenty and after a few trials you will find that the deduction of thirteen almost becomes automatic.

THE SLIP FORCE

Just as we gave you more than one way to control a selected card we think we should give you an alternative method of forcing a card. The Slip Force which we shall describe is easy to do and absolutely certain in its action. It is therefore very popular with amateur magicians, who generally do it very badly. We shall give you a method which is absolutely undetectable because the secret action is entirely covered by a natural movement.

You secretly place the card you desire to force upon the top of the pack and you false shuffle so as to leave the card there.

You state that you wish to have a card selected entirely by chance and that you will ask a lady to thrust the bottom card, face up, into the pack at any point she desires. You remove the bottom card as you speak and hand it, face up, to one of the ladies. You hold the pack in the palm of the left hand, face down, with the thumb across the back of the top card and the four fingers against its right side. and you ask the lady to thrust the corner of her card into the end of the pack wherever she desires. When she has done so you bring the right hand over the pack and grasp all the cards, above her face-up one, between the right third finger at the far end and the thumb at the near end, and you open the pack to the right at that point as if it were a book, the left thumb moving away to permit this, as shown in Figure 13. With the cards in this position

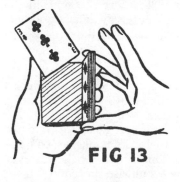

FIG 13

you will find that the tips of the left second and third fingers rest against the back of the top card of the pack (the force card). Please notice also that the right first and second fingers are unoccupied. Now you do several things at the same time and you must practise them so that you can do them without any excessive haste yet with all the actions blending together into one smooth motion. First you draw your hands back a little to free the pack from the face up card held by the lady. Then you press upon the top card with the left middle fingers and you turn the right hand a little towards yourself. The left fingers drag the top card off the upper packet as the right hand carries the latter away and the card is slipped, like a flash, upon the lower packet. The right hand, carrying the upper packet, moves in an arc to the face-up card the lady holds, grasps it between the unoccupied first and second fingers, and takes it from her. The left hand is immediately extended towards the lady with the lower packet as you say : " We will not use the card above, which we have all seen, but the one below." The lady accordingly takes the top card of lower packet.

The superiority of our method over those generally used and described lies in the action of taking the face up card from the lady with the hand that holds the top packet and thus giving us a natural reason for moving this hand away, a movement which entirely masks the slipping of the force card from the top to the centre.

The Slip Force will require a little practice before you can do it well but there is no great difficulty about it provided that your hands are reasonably well kept.

WITH A FORCED CARD

Many remarkable effects can be produced when you have learned to force, but the ability to ensure the selection of a certain card must be used with discretion and not abused. I think it was Mr. Jean Hugard, Australian-born author of a number of fine American books on conjuring, who first remarked that the amateur, when he forces a card, is apt to reveal the fact by his unwise procedure. Instead of continuing as he would have done with a freely selected card he hands the pack to the " selector " and tells him to replace the card himself and to shuffle the cards well. This, of course, is wrong. Proceed in your usual way. Have the card returned as you always do and shuffle the pack yourself. Afterwards, if you wish, you may hand the cards to a spectator for shuffling.

We will give you an excellent trick as an example of the way to use a forced card.

First you glance at the bottom card of the pack, remember its name, and shuffle it to the top. Let us suppose that this card is the ace of Diamonds. Force this ace upon one of the

spectators by means of either of the methods we have taught
you. Ask the selector to show the card to the company and
then let him replace it in the pack. Shuffle the pack well and
then, as if it were an afterthought, ask him if he would like
to shuffle also. When he has shuffled take the pack from him
and say : " I want to find the Joker. I suppose, by the way,
it was not the Joker you chose ? No ! Good." You fan the
pack between your hands and you find, first the forced card
(the ace of Diamonds) and then the Joker. You remove the
Joker and throw it down upon the table. Then you cut the
pack to take the ace to the top and you immediately shuffle
the pack again, this time shuffling the ace to the bottom.
You put the pack down on the table by the side of the Joker.

Now you ask the selector of the card to cut the pack, and by
a gesture you indicate that you wish him to put the part
cut down beside the other half. You drop the Joker face up
upon the original top portion of the pack and you complete
the cut by picking up the bottom half and dropping it on top
of the Joker.

Now you remind the audience of the course of events. A
card has been selected and replaced in the pack which has been
shuffled by the selector. The position of the card in the pack
is therefore entirely a matter of chance. The selector has cut
the pack and the cut has been marked by the Joker. " There
are some things that can only be described as remarkable
coincidences until they happen again and again . . . and then
one calls them magic." As you say the last words you take
hold of the Joker and with it turn over the top half of the
pack to reveal the selected card.

The recapitulation of events in this case has served two
purposes. It has " built up " the effect and it has allowed an
interval to elapse between the cutting of the pack and the
ultimate disclosure of the result, an interval which has given
time for the details of the somewhat irregular cutting procedure
to have faded from the spectators' minds.

THE CARD UNDER THE CARPET

But it is when we use an extra card, a duplicate card, that the force really comes into its own and, by its means, a selected card is apparently made to fly from the pack and reappear elsewhere. Sometimes two or three cards are forced and made to reappear in some piece of apparatus. Actually, of course, it is the duplicates that reappear. We are not including tricks with apparatus in this Handbook but we will briefly mention some of the best things of this sort, which may be purchased from dealers in magical equipment.

There are various kinds of frames which may be shown empty and will yet " produce " selected cards. In our companion volume *A Handbook of Conjuring* you will find the description of a trick with a small picture frame and a number of postcards which may also be done with a playing card. There is a special sword which, when plunged into a pack of cards which has been thrown into the air, will produce a duplicate of the chosen card, impaled upon its point. Truly an astonishing effect. There are various forms of the Rising Card Trick also, in which selected cards rise out of the pack while it stands in a glass or in a simple piece of apparatus.

For the amateur performer the trick we shall now describe is, in many ways, equal to any of these apparatus tricks and has the advantage over all of them that it needs no expensive equipment. You will need only an extra card taken from another pack having the same patterned back. (When you buy your cards, always buy two packs at a time, so that you will have plenty of different duplicate cards available. There is an old story told amongst conjurers of a professional appearing at a theatre who had the nine of clubs "chosen" from the pack twice nightly all the week !)

You will also need momentary access, alone, to the room in which you will be performing, some time beforehand, so that you may slip your duplicate card under the corner of the carpet, or under a rug, at the part of the room which you will occupy when you do your turn.

Now, in the course of your performance you look through

the pack and locate the duplicate of the card under the carpet. You cut the pack to bring this card to the top and you remove the Joker as the ostensible reason for looking through the pack. You hand the Joker to one of the spectators and invite him to thrust the corner of it into the pack. You use the slip force to have your duplicated card selected. You allow a second spectator to select a card in exactly the same way, by thrusting the Joker into the pack, but this time you do not slip the top card. You allow a real choice to be made. However you must proceed in *exactly* the same way as you did when you forced the card.

Now you have the two cards replaced in the pack and you bring them both to the top by one of the methods previously described, and you false shuffle to leave the cards there. The duplicate of the card under the carpet should be the second card from the top of the pack.

You go down on one knee and put the pack down on the carpet near to the spot beneath which the concealed card lies. You ask the person who drew the freely chosen card to name it, and you pick up the pack and throw it down upon the carpet so that the card he names appears face up on top of it. (See the trick called "The Revolution" which we described in connection with "Think of a Number" in Part I.)

You turn this card face down again and ask the other selector to name his card, the forced one. Once more you pick up the pack and slap it down upon the carpet, but, as you do not slide the top card off the pack, nothing happens. At this you must appear to be very surprised. You pick up the pack and slap it down again, still without result. You turn the pack towards yourself and, frowning furiously, you look through it as though you were seeking the card. Suddenly you smile and say "Ah! I must have slapped it down too hard", and you turn back the carpet to reveal the chosen card!

THE ONE WAY PACK

We now introduce you to another principle which has almost unlimited possibilities if it is used with imagination.

If you will examine a pack of cards of the kind which has a geometrical pattern, or a " wall-paper " pattern to its back, you will observe at first sight that the pattern is the same whichever way the card is turned. We will now ask you to examine the cards more carefully, comparing one with another and we shall be very surprised if, after close inspection, you do not find some slight difference in the patterns at the two ends of the pack. The difference, no doubt, will be very small, such as a leaf with a sharp point at one end and one with a round point at the other, or a trifling difference in the position of two dots, but, nevertheless, the difference will be easy to discern when you know what to look for, and it will be repeated in every card of the pack. Some excellent cards may be found for this purpose which have a check design of small squares, in which the corner square at one end is white while that at the opposite end is red or blue, according to the pack.

Now, if you arrange the cards so that they all point the same way, that is to say so that all the pointed leaves or all the white corner squares are at the same end, you have a " one way pack." Take any card from this pack and turn it round and, however much the pack is shuffled you can always find that card by looking at the backs.

The brightly coloured bridge cards, so popular today, which bear on their backs pictures of kittens, pretty girls, or Swiss mountains, according to taste, are all " one way packs " but cannot be used for our purpose because they are so *too obviously*. We can introduce another stratagem, however, in order to use them. First you mix all the cards so that some of the kittens for example, are head ups and others are tails up, and then you make a minute mark in one corner of each card. You will now have a one way pack which is independent of the back design, and you will always be able to find a card that has been reversed in this pack by the position of your mark. The marks may be made with coloured ink to match the colour of the cards or may be simple pencil dots ; or you may remove a tiny fragment of coloured surface, with the point of a sharp knife, to leave a white spot on the card.

We will give you two or three tricks to illustrate the use of this principle.

ONE WAY ELIMINATION

Using a one way pack, all the cards of which are pointing in the same direction, you spread it between your hands for a card to be selected. When the card has been taken you close the pack and hold it in your left hand while you ask the chooser to show his choice to the rest of the company. You watch carefully to see how he handles the card and if he turns it end for end. If he does not turn the card round you take the pack in your right hand, grasping it by the far end, and spread it in a fan with a twist of the fingers, asking him to replace the card. Thus you have reversed the pack and his card will be pointing in a different direction from all the others. On the other hand, if you see him turn his card, you fan the pack in your left hand without reversing it.

You may now shuffle the pack and let the selector shuffle also, after which you divide the pack into two heaps and invite him to guess which one contains his card. You take the heap he indicates and fan it between your hands, showing him the faces and looking at the backs yourself. You look for the reversed card, of course. If you do not find it you say, " I think you guessed wrong that time " and discard the heap, but if you do find it you congratulate him upon having guessed correctly.

Now you give the half pack a shuffle and divide it into two portions again, asking him to guess once more which packet contains his card. Again you fan the cards of the packet he chooses, congratulate him if he is correct, and discard the packet that does not contain the card.

The twelve or so cards that remain you shuffle and divide into two portions. Holding one lot in each hand you spread them so that you can see the backs sufficiently well to distinguish the reversed card, and you ask the assisting spectator to guess " left or right." Again you tell him if he is right or wrong and you discard the " wrong " cards.

You continue thus until you have only one card left, which proves to be the selected one.

THE TRANSPOSED CARD

With all the cards of your one way pack pointing in the same direction, you shuffle it well and put it down upon the table. Now you cut the pack into two portions which you place one on either side of the table. To do this you grasp the pack by its ends between the second fingers and thumbs of each hand, the left hand grasping the bottom half and the right hand the top half of the pack. You separate the hands, each holding half the pack, and put the halves down on opposite sides of the table. You will find that this naturally leaves the one way backs of the two halves pointing in opposite directions.

You retire from the table and invite a spectator to remove a card from one of the heaps, to show it to the company, and to put it within the other heap. Then you ask him to shuffle both the heaps and replace them on the table.

Now you return to the table and reassemble the pack. In doing so you reverse the movements you made when you cut the pack. That is to say, you grasp each heap by its end, bring them in front of you, and place one on top of the other. All the cards will now be pointing in the same direction except the transposed card.

There are many ways in which you might complete the trick but we will suggest that you use the following. Take the cards and begin to look through them, searching for the reversed back. Cut the pack anywhere and remove the top card. Look at this card and name it, saying, for example, " Was the selected card the ten of Clubs ? " On receiving the negative response drop the card on to the table, allowing the spectators to get a fleeting glimpse of its face, so that they may see that it is, indeed, the card you named ; but do not deliberately show it to them.

Now find the reversed card and cut that to the top. Look at the card which, for convenience of description, we will suppose is the Queen of Spades, and say " Was the selected card the nine of Diamonds ? " Drop the card on to the table on the right hand side of the first one, but do not allow the face of the card to be seen. You must remember the name by which you miscalled this card.

Cut the pack a third time and take the new top card. Look at it and name it, saying, for example, " Was it the two of Clubs ? " Again drop the card upon the table, to the right of the last one, without letting its face be seen.

Say, " Three attempts and three failures. It is not the . . . . " pick up the left hand card and glance at his face, then replace it without showing it and continue your sentence . . . . " the ten of Clubs or . . . . " look at the centre card, again, needless to say, without showing it . . . . " the nine of Diamonds " (miscalling it again) " or . . . . " look at the right hand card, this time tilting it a little so that its face may be seen and naming it . . . . " the two of Clubs ? Too bad ! "

Ask a lady to choose one of the three cards and, by means of the equivocal force with which you should now be familiar, interpret her selection to mean the centre card and replace the other two in the pack. Now announce that you will make the previously selected card change places with the one the lady has now chosen. Ask for the name of the selected card. Command the cards to change places. Make a crackling noise with your thumb against the edge of the pack and ask someone to turn up the card upon the table . . . . and there is the selected card, the Queen of Spades !

You have there a fine example of the real art of conjuring, an art in which acting is of far more importance than dexterity.

IN YOUR HANDS

You secretly reverse the top half of your one way pack, which you put down upon the table. You cut the pack, cutting only about a quarter of the cards, and you complete the cut. The result of these actions is that the centre of the pack points in the opposite direction to the rest of the cards.

You invite a spectator to take the pack in his own hands while you retire to the side of the room. You request him to take a card from the centre of the pack, to show it to the company, to replace it on the top of the pack, to cut the pack and complete the cut, and, finally, to replace the cards upon the table.

The selected card will now be in the centre of the pack pointing in the opposite direction to all its neighbours.

Spread the cards in a face up over-lapping row upon the table and ask one of the spectators to indicate which portion of the pack contains the card. Remove about a dozen cards from the point indicated and spread them in a fan, holding it with the backs of the cards towards yourself. You will be able to see the position of the selected card quite easily because of its reversed back.

Ask the selector to concentrate his mind upon his card. Run your finger backwards and forwards along the top of the fan once or twice and then stop at the selected card, draw it from the fan, and hand it to him.

THE FIVE CARD TRICK

This is, in the Author's personal opinion, the best trick that can be done with a one way pack.

You begin by giving the pack to be shuffled and, when you receive it back, you ask a spectator to thrust a pencil into the centre of the pack and push out a small packet of cards. You pull these cards out and drop them on the top of the pack. Then you take the top five cards in your right hand and spread them into a fan, which you show to one of the spectators, asking him to think of one of them. You hand him also a slip of paper and a pencil and ask him to write the name of his card upon it, to fold it, and to hand it to another spectator. You turn away while he writes so that it is impossible for you to see. You ask the second spectator to look at the name of the card upon the paper and then to mentally select a second one from the five that you hold. You ask him to write the name of his card on the slip of paper for the sake of the record. Throughout these proceedings you take care to hold the five cards so that the spectators can see that you do not look at the faces of them.

Now you replace the five cards in different parts of the pack, quite naturally *reversing them*, and you hand the pack to someone to shuffle.

When you receive the pack back you take a small number of cards from the top, six, seven, or eight, and spread them in a fan. You watch for a reversed card amongst them. You show these cards to each of the assisting spectators asking if the cards of which they thought are amongst them. Should they both say " No " you put these cards aside and take another small batch. You keep watch for the cards that are reversed in the pack and take care never to include more than one such card in any fan. So, when either of the choosers tells you that his card is amongst those you hold you know at once that it is the reversed one. After some hesitation, acting as though you were " mind reading " you pick out the correct card from the fan. You carry on thus to find the second selected card.

THE PACK REVEALS IT

We shall now leave the One Way Pack to give you severa tricks which depend upon a pre-arrangement of the cards. Some astonishing effects may be produced by this means.

You arrange your pack so that the top card is a ten, the second a nine, the third an eight, and so on down to the tenth card, which will be an ace. The suits do not matter, it is only the numerical sequence 10, 9, 8, 7, 6, 5, 4, 3, 2, 1 which is required. Make a little bend or crimp in one corner of the Ace so that you will be able to cut at that card (see " The Corner Crimp " in Part I).

False shuffle the pack to leave the top stock (your ten arranged cards) undisturbed, and then invite one of the company to select a card and to show it to the others. Cut at the crimp for the replacement of the selected card, drop the cut back on top of it, and then false shuffle again, leaving the top eleven cards undisturbed.

Now spread the pack upon the table so that the top twelve or fifteen cards lie in an overlapping line, and ask one of the company to touch any one of the cards thus exposed. Turn up the card that is touched and call the number of spots upon it. Count that number of cards along the row and turn up the next one . . . . the selected card.

ODD AND EVEN

We have previously shown you how you may arrange a few cards in the course of one trick for the purpose of another, and we shall now give you a trick in which, with colossal audacity, the conjurer arranges the whole pack in front of his audience. But it will be, of course, quite a simple arrangement.

The effect of the trick is similar to that of " The Transposed Card " which we described when we were discussing the One Way Pack, but the present trick may be performed with any cards. First you hand the pack to a spectator for thorough shuffling and, when you receive it back, you cut it into two equal portions. You invite a spectator, while you turn away, to take any card from either heap, show it to the company, and bury it in the other heap. You then direct him to reassemble the pack by placing the two heaps together, to cut and to complete the cut.

This having been done you take the pack and look through it very carefully, You appear to make some mental calculation and then you remove one card and put it face down upon the table. You ask the name of the transposed card and then you turn over the card on the table. You have failed !

" I can't understand this," you say. " Will you try again ? " Once more you cut the pack into two halves. You turn away while the spectator takes any card from either heap and buries it in the other. He reassembles the pack, cuts, and completes the cut. All this while you stand with your back to the table. You turn now and look through the pack and, after a little hesitation, you remove one card and put it down upon the table. You ask the name of the transposed card and you turn over the one on the table. You are right !

With the knowledge of conjuring which you have gained from this Handbook you will be rather suspicious of that preliminary failure. In fact it is the secret of the trick. The first time you look through the pack you separate the cards between the odd ones and the even ones. As you pass the cards from the left hand into the right hand you put all the even cards in front and all the odd ones behind. (The odd cards, of course, are the Ace, three, five, seven, nine, Jack, and King . . . . the others are the even ones.) When you have the pack thus divided, you crimp the corner of the even card on the face of the pack, the bottom card, and then run through once more until you come to the first odd card. You throw this card down upon the table and then cut at the dividing point between odd and even, thus taking the crimped card to the centre.

Now, when you " try again ", you simply cut the pack at the crimped card and thus divide it into two approximately equal parts, one containing all the odd and the other all the even cards. You will now have no difficulty in finding the transposed card, one even card amongst all the odd ones or one odd card amongst the even ones.

Bear in mind that there is always a *possibility* that you may pick the correct card at the first attempt. In such a case conceal your own astonishment and take credit for the miracle you have performed . . . . with all due modesty, of course !

WITH TWO PACKS

One of the two packs which you will use for this experiment must be previously arranged so that the spot values of any two consecutive cards, when added together, will total either fourteen or fifteen. You will have to discard two aces to do this, so that the pack will consist of only fifty cards. The following is an example of how the beginning of the pack might run :

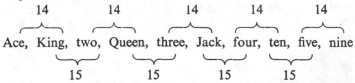

and so on. The suits of course, do not matter. Have this pack in your pocket, in its case, and commence the trick with the other one, which is without any arrangement.

You first shuffle the pack and then you spread it between your hands and ask someone to select a card. As you pass the cards from hand to hand you secretly count them, and you keep a break beneath the fourteenth one. When a card has been selected you close the pack and slip the tip of your little finger into the break to hold the division beneath the fourteenth card. You ask the chooser to show his card to the company and then you cut at the break for him to return it to the pack. You drop the cut back on top of his card, deliberately square up the pack, and execute your top stock shuffle. The selected card will be the fifteenth in the pack. You hand this pack to a spectator to hold, first, as a wise precaution, putting an elastic band around it in case he should be seized with a sudden urge to shuffle. Always be careful in such cases, particularly with habitual card players, many of whom automatically shuffle a pack when it is handed to them.

You now produce the second pack, which you remove from its case and casually cut once or twice. This cutting does not spoil the order of the cards. A pack of cards that has been arranged in sequence is very much like one of those lines of marching caterpillars of which one occasionally reads. Divert the leader from his course so that he veers round the trunk of a tree and begins to follow the last in line and all the caterpillars will march endlessly round and round the tree until exhaustion overcomes them or you divert them once again. It is thus with the arranged pack. The top card is always ready to follow the bottom one and both of them are prepared to become middle units. Cutting the pack, so long as the cut is properly completed, only creates new top and bottom cards, new first and last caterpillars, without altering the sequence of the units of the pack. But to return to our trick.

Hand the pack to another spectator and ask him to cut it wherever he wishes and to remove two cards. Take the pack from him and ask him to add together the spot value of the two cards he has removed, explaining that Jacks count as eleven, Queens as twelve, and Kings as thirteen. Ask him then to announce the answer to his piece of arithmetic which, because of the arrangement of the cards, is bound to be either fourteen or fifteen.

Turn to the spectator who holds the other pack and ask him, if the number is fourteen, to deal fourteen cards from his pack and to place the fifteenth in his pocket. If, however, the number is fifteen, ask him to count down in the pack and to put the fifteenth card in his pocket.

Pause now for your necessary recapitulation which will build up the effect, which is truly astonishing. One person has selected a card which has been shuffled back into the pack. A second person has taken two cards at random from another pack and added their values together to produce an haphazard figure. A third person has put into his pocket the card standing at that number in the shuffled pack.

Quietly ask the name of the selected card and then request the spectator to remove it from his pocket.

EIGHT KINGS

There are various ways in which a pack may be arranged so that the conjurer can remember the complete order of the cards, from the first to last, and so that the sight of one card will tell him the name of the next. This leads to a host of interesting possibilities which we can only touch in passing in the course of this Handbook.

One of the oldest and simplest ideas is that known as the

" Eight Kings " because the order of the cards is remembered by means of the following jingle :—

> Eight Kings threatened to save
> Ninety-five ladies for one sick Knave.

These cryptic lines are easily remembered and will recall to you the order of eight, King, three, ten, two, seven (save), nine, five, Queen, four, Ace (one), six, Jack (knave).

You must now fix upon an arrangement of suits. You may take the Bridge order, Clubs, Diamonds, Hearts, Spades, or one of alternating colours, such as Clubs, Hearts, Spades, Diamonds, which can be remembered by another ancient formula, CHaSeD, in which the capitals give the suits. Let us suppose you decide upon the latter.

To arrange your pack you first sort it out into the four suits. Now take one of the Clubs, let us suppose it is the six. You remember your lines about the sick Knave and you place on the face up *six* of Clubs the *knave* of Hearts. You return to the commencement of your memorized lines and you find the *eight* of Spades, then the *King* of Diamonds, the *three* of Clubs, the *ten* of Hearts, the *two* of Spades, the *seven* of Diamonds, and you carry on in this way until you reach the last card of the pack, which will be the Ace of Diamonds. If you wish to include the Joker in the pack you may do so provided you take care to remember at exactly what point in the arrangement you have placed it. It is advisable always to have it at the same point.

Naturally, with the pack arranged thus, you can always tell what card has been taken from it by looking at the one that was above it. The best way to do this is to cut the pack at the point from which the card is drawn and then to secretly glance at the bottom card. Then if, when the card is replaced, you undercut the pack, that is, draw off the bottom half and have the chosen card replaced beneath it, you will restore the pack to the complete arrangement. A better use for the arranged pack is given in the trick that follows.

THREE CARD DIVINATION

With your cards arranged in the Eight Kings order you invite three spectators each to choose one from the pack, which you spread between your hands in the usual fashion. As each person selects his card you open the pack a little to allow him to withdraw it and then, with your left thumb, you pull the card which was beneath the chosen one about an inch to the left. You press down a little on the edge of this card and tilt it up with your thumb so that you can slide the top portion of the pack beneath it as you close the cards. The card next in sequence to the chosen one thus becomes the top card of the pack. You do this each time a card is selected so that, at the conclusion, you have three cards on the top of the pack which follow, in the Eight Kings order, the cards which have been selected. As each card is drawn you ask the choosers to put them into their pockets without looking at them, " so that there can be no question of thought reading being the simple solution to the problem in progress."

When you have slipped the three cards to the top of the pack you false shuffle by simply drawing off the three cards, one by one, and then shuffling the rest of the pack on top of them.

You are now able to " divine " the name of the three cards in the spectators pockets, " three cards which nobody knows." You fan the cards towards yourself and pretend to study them. Naturally you have only to look at the bottom card of the pack and go one backwards in your arrangement to know the name of the first selected card. For example, if the bottom card is the five of Diamonds .... you know that a nine always precedes a five and a spade a diamond. Then the first selected card is the nine of spades. Simply ask the spectator to put his hand into his pocket and hand you the nine of Spades !

In exactly the same way the second card from the bottom will give you the second selected card and the third from the bottom the last selected one.

SI STEBBINS' ARRANGEMENT

Another method of arranging a pack, of American origin, is known by the name of its inventor, Si Stebbins, and is, perhaps, superior to the Eight Kings arrangement. It is very simple and may be summed up in the words " change the suit and add three." Thus, supposing you are using the Bridge order of the suits and you begin your arrangement with the Ace of Clubs, you would follow that card with the four of Diamonds, seven of Hearts, ten of Spades, King of Clubs, three of Diamonds, six of Hearts, and so on, always adding three points to the last card and changing the suit. Your pack which started with the Ace of Clubs would finish with the Jack of Spades.

All the tricks done with the Eight Kings arrangement may be performed with the Si Stebbins' pack and to them we would add the following excellent trick which makes use of the fact that, in this arrangement, the cards of each suit run in descending order, that is to say, the King of Clubs is followed four cards later by the Queen, and four cards later still by the Jack of Clubs, and so on down to the Ace. And this is so for all the suits.

ONE IN FIVE

You seat a spectator at the table and place the pack, arranged in Si Stebbins' order, in front of him. You turn your back and instruct him to cut the pack anywhere he wishes and to complete the cut. You ask him if he is satisfied that the cut was made at random or if he would wish to cut again. You make sure that he is satisfied that he has had a free choice. You ask him then to look at the card he cut, the new top card of the pack, to show it to the company, and to put it face down upon the table. You then ask him to deal four more cards on to the table and to put the pack into his pocket. Finally you ask him to mix up the five cards on the table and then to arrange them in one row.

You turn back to the table and examine the cards one after

the other. Finally you pick up one of the cards and hand it to the assisting spectator. It is the chosen card.

If you will go over the action of the trick again, bearing in mind the manner in which the pack is arranged you will understand that of the five cards on the table two will be of the same suit and the others of the three other suits. The selected card will always be the higher of the two cards of the same suit.

READING THE PACK

The ancient trick of reading all the cards of the pack without seeing their faces may be done, of course, with the arranged pack, although it would be unwise to read too many cards because of the risk that the regular rotation of the suits might be noticed by an observant spectator. However, by the use of a little ingenuity an excellent trick can be made of this feat which can well follow some other effect with an arranged pack.

A little preparation will be necessary. Pinned to the back of your trousers, underneath your coat, you must have a little spring paper clip. In your right hand upper-most vest pocket you have six cards taken from another pack with the same back design. You must remember the names of these six cards and their order. If you always use the same six cards for this trick their names will soon be familiar to you.

First you false shuffle the pack by the method we described in Part I under the heading of " False Shuffling IV ", leaving a good stock undisturbed on the top of the pack after you have cut it. You hold the pack behind your back with both hands while you tell your story of the possibility of card reading by sightless vision. While you are talking you must do several things and you should therefore take the pains to determine beforehand exactly what you will say, so that you will be able to talk without hesitation while you are thinking of something else. The first thing you do is to put five cards in the clip under the back of your coat. You keep your arms pressed closely to your sides while you do this and use only your hands and wrists so that no movement of your elbows will be seen to warn the spectators that you are busily at work. Next you palm the top card of the pack in your right hand and you take in the same hand the bottom card which you bring forward as you say, " Notice please that I do not hold the card up like this and then name it. I name the cards while they are still behind my back and normal vision of any sort is quite impossible."

You replace the card on the bottom of the pack behind your back but, just as the hand retires with the card, you glance at the palmed one and, from it, you at once know the names of the five cards in the clip and the cards that are on the top of the pack. You put the palmed card on the bottom of the pack also, as by omitting to read this card you break the sequence of the cards you do read, naming two small batches instead of one long series.

You now name the top card of the pack (it follows the palmed one in the arrangement) and bring it forward and drop it upon the table. You may then read three more cards from the top, fairly rapidly, in the same way. For example, supposing that you are using the Si Stebbins' arrangement, if the palmed card was the King of Clubs the cards read will be the three of Diamonds, six of Hearts, nine of Spades, and Queen of Clubs.

At this point you bring the pack forward again and hand it to someone to shuffle. On receiving it back you put it behind your back again and quickly pull the five cards from the clip and add them to the top of the pack. Now you must think backwards from the King of Clubs . . . . ten of Spades, seven of Hearts, four of Diamonds, Ace of Clubs, Jack of Spades . . . . and you are ready to call the names of the five cards, beginning with the top one, the Jack of Spades. If you think it desirable you may produce the cards in an irregular order. You call the first two cards as you stand facing the spectators with the cards behind you. Then turn sideways to them and turn up the next three cards as you name them.

Again hand the pack to someone to shuffle and remark that some people sometimes think that it is not really a question of sightless vision but of a superior sense of touch. Take the pack back and drop it into your coat pocket as you say that you will name the cards without either seeing or touching them. Name the first of the six cards in your upper vest pocket. Thrust your hand into your coat pocket and apparently bring out from it the card you have named but really take the card from the upper vest pocket. (You will remember that we used this idea also in the trick called "Thought Divined" in Part I). Name the second card of your memorized six and remove it in the same way. Then name the remaining four cards one after the other and remove them very rapidly from the pocket, bringing the trick to a brisk termination.

PREPARED CARDS

There are so many different kinds of special cards and prepared packs which may be made, or may be purchased from the dealers in conjuring apparatus, that it is quite impossible to deal with them adequately in the space at our disposal and, in any case, we strongly advise you to use none of them until, at least, your experience of conjuring is sufficient to enable you to make a sound judgment of the merits and demerits of each one of them. You will also find that in your early conjuring years your chief opportunities to perform will be found in the homes of your friends, perhaps after a game of cards, and you will naturally use the cards that you find there rather than produce a pack of your own.

One of the oldest ideas in connection with special cards is to have in the pack one card which is a fraction longer or wider than all the others. Many makers of playing cards enclose in the outer wrapping of their packs a specimen card, either a blank card, an extra joker, or a bridge score card. These specimens often differ in size very slightly from the cards they accompany and will make excellent long or wide cards. Such a card can always be found in the shuffled pack by the feel of the fingers and can be used as a key card. If a selected card is replaced under the wide or long card, cutting he pack at that point will take the chosen card to the top.

A later and better idea is the short or narrow card made by taking a minute shaving from the end or side of a card. The short or narrow card is better than the long one because it cannot be accidentally discovered by a spectator who handles the pack. To find the short card you take the pack in the left hand and place the right hand fingers on the far end and the thumb upon the near end. Now you run the finger tips across the ends of the cards, raising them a little and releasing them one by one in a steady stream, when a slight pause in the even falling of the cards will tell you when you have reached the short one. A little practice will enable you to stop with accuracy at the short card. A narrow card is found in a similar way by running the thumb across the side of the pack.

Another idea, now fallen somewhat into disuse in this country but still popular with continental conjurers, is the bisauté pack which our American friends call the " stripper deck." The sides of this pack are trimmed to make all the cards very slightly wedge shaped, slightly wider at one end than at the other. When all the cards are arranged so that the wide ends are together the pack appears to be unprepared yet, if any card is reversed in the pack, that is to say, turned end for end, it can readily be found since it becomes a " wide " card at the narrow end of the pack. By holding the pack by the sides at one end, and running the fingers of the other hand down its long edges, a reversed card may be drawn out of the pack. Any number of cards reversed in this way may be drawn out thus with one action and put either on the top or the bottom of the pack, and it is this stripping of the cards from the pack which has suggested its American name, the stripper deck. (Various old English words like " deck " now no longer used in English have survived in the American language.) The bisauté pack is used in very much the same way as the One Way Pack, being turned round after the cards have been selected so that they will be replaced in reversed position. Most of the conjuring dealers who sell the stripper deck include with it very full instructions.

There are various ways in which the cards may be marked

so that they can be identified as readily from their backs as from their faces. Marked cards, or " reader decks " as the Americans call them, may be purchased ready made, or you may make your own. Red backed cards will be marked with red ink, and blue backed ones with blue ink, so that the markings will be practically invisible to anyone who does not know what to look for and where to look. The backs of most cards show a pattern in white upon a blue or red back-ground. The pattern generally consists of leaves, scrolls, dots, or points, all of which may be shortened, altered, or obliterated by a pen stroke. One of the best methods of marking consists in deciding upon twelve such points and to alter or erase the point that gives the value of the card. That is to say the seventh point will be altered on all the four sevens and the twelfth point on all the four Queens, while the kings will be left unmarked. Three further points will be required to give the suits, the clubs, diamonds, and hearts being marked while the spades are left untouched. So the only unmarked card in the pack will be the King of Spades. The cards can also be marked in this way by being pricked with a needle, in which case they are " read " by feeling with the finger tips, as a blind man reads braille. This is not an accomplishment you will learn in a few hours. Needless to say in all systems of marking the cards are marked at both ends.

A very good trick pack would be one consisting of marked cards arranged in Si Stebbins' order. When a card is drawn from this pack a glance at the back one of its former neighbours will give the name of the card withdrawn.

Various trick packs are sold, made with long and short cards, cards stuck together in pairs, cards with false indices, cards that are all alike, double backed cards, double faced cards, and an infinity of ingenious ideas. We advise you to have nothing to do with any of them. Most of them have been invented for only one purpose, to sell to uninformed amateurs and clumsy dabblers in conjuring.

There are also some ingenious mechanical changing cards which, if intelligently used, can find a place in a conjuring

programme, such as the beautifully made "moving pip
cards" which can change from, say, fives to sevens. By
simply moving a tiny lever you may make two pips detach
themselves from the others and move to occupy the vacant
spaces on the card.

Occasionally the playing card manufacturers, prompted by
the more ingenious and irresponsible members of the fraternity,
give us some excellent joke cards which are worth collecting
and using occasionally. Imagine the feelings of a spectator who
finds that he has "chosen" from the pack the fifteen of Diamonds or the seven and a half of Clubs !

IN CONCLUSION

We should not be doing our duty to the reader if we left him
without a few words of general advice and counsel. It would
have been better, perhaps, to have done this at the beginning
rather than at the end of our Handbook, but we know well
that Prefaces are never read, and hungry diners seldom pause
to read articles on dietetics.

You may have discovered already, by grim experience, that
all conjuring tricks, even the most simple, require a certain
amount of practice before they can be done with any success.
If they are to be done really well they need a considerable
amount of practice. The chief thing is to moderate your
enthusiasm and not rush off to show your new tricks to the
neighbours before you have learned them thoroughly. And to
learn a trick thoroughly it is best to proceed by regular and
well defined stages.

First, read our description of the trick at least twice and
make sure that you follow our explanation and understand
exactly what you must do and precisely what the effect of the
trick will be to the spectators. Next make sure that you can
do, *with ease*, all the manipulations which the trick requires.
If, for example, you have to false shuffle the pack, you must
practise this shuffle until you can do it without thinking about
it, just as when you shuffle the cards fairly. If, after that, you

have to palm a card, you must also practise your palming until you can do it as easily as you can sign your name.

Having made sure that all the different secret actions are well within your ability to do, you can begin to perform the trick *to yourself*, as a whole, first with the book in front of you and then from memory. After doing it half a dozen times you should be ready to advance another step.

Sit down in an armchair and spend half an hour thinking about the trick and considering what you will say when you are doing it. We have given you numerous lines in the Handbook which may serve as examples of the kind of talk you need, but we have refrained, deliberately, from giving you too much talk because it is essential that what you say should come naturally from you, and should suit your character and personality. Make a few notes of suitable " lines of patter ", including any jokes that may occur to you as apt and suitable, but do not upset yourself by racking your brains for witticisms. A conjurer does not have to be a comedian.

You will now be able to REHEARSE your trick, combining words and actions, and going through it several times. Stand before your wardrobe mirror and do the trick to yourself a number of times, watching the expression of your face and checking generally on your acting of the little play, for every conjuring trick is a play in miniature. In this rehearsal you must talk *out loud* as if you were actually doing the trick to a company of spectators. It is not sufficient to simply mutter the words to yourself. The rehearsal must be a real attempt to perform the trick exactly as you will perform it, soon, to a " real live audience."

We have said that a trick is a miniature play and, if it is to be a successful play, it must be acted with conviction. When you order a card to fly from the centre of the pack to the top you must express your command as though you were convinced of its necessity and sure of its efficacy. It is only by adequately rehearsing your words and actions that you will be able to do this.

When you have conscientiously rehearsed you may face

your audience with confidence and assurance. You will probably feel rather nervous but your nervousness will not effect your ability. We hope indeed, that you will feel nervous, for it is always a sign of the artist to be a little highly strung, and unless you have something of the artist in you, you will never make a good conjurer.

BIBLIOGRAPHY

SELECTED AND ADVANCED WORKS

Erdnase, S. W. *The Expert at the Card Table.* Chas. T. Powner Co., Chicago, 1944.

Hilliard, J. N. *Card Magic.* (forms part of separate book, *Greater Magic.*) C. W. Jones, Minneapolis, Minn., 1945.

Hugard, J., *ed. Encyclopedia of Card Tricks.* Max Holden, New York City, 1937.

Hugard, J. and Fred Braue. *Expert Card Technique.* G. Starke, New York City, 1950.

Hugard, J. and Fred Braue. *The Royal Road to Card Magic.* Harper and Bros., New York-London, 1948.

Young, M. N. *Hobby Magic.* Trilon Press, Div. of Magazine & Periodical Pntg. & Pub. Co., Inc., Brooklyn, N. Y., 1950.

INDEX

A CATALOG OF
SELECTED DOVER BOOKS
IN ALL FIELDS OF INTEREST

A CATALOG OF SELECTED DOVER BOOKS IN ALL FIELDS OF INTEREST

CONCERNING THE SPIRITUAL IN ART, Wassily Kandinsky. Pioneering work by father of abstract art. Thoughts on color theory, nature of art. Analysis of earlier masters. 12 illustrations. 80pp. of text. 5⅜ × 8½. 23411-8 Pa. $2.50

LEONARDO ON THE HUMAN BODY, Leonardo da Vinci. More than 1200 of Leonardo's anatomical drawings on 215 plates. Leonardo's text, which accompanies the drawings, has been translated into English. 506pp. 8⅜ × 11¾. 24483-0 Pa. $10.95

GOBLIN MARKET, Christina Rossetti. Best-known work by poet comparable to Emily Dickinson, Alfred Tennyson. With 46 delightfully grotesque illustrations by Laurence Housman. 64pp. 4 × 6¾. 24516-0 Pa. $2.50

THE HEART OF THOREAU'S JOURNALS, edited by Odell Shepard. Selections from *Journal*, ranging over full gamut of interests. 228pp. 5⅜ × 8½. 20741-2 Pa. $4.50

MR. LINCOLN'S CAMERA MAN: MATHEW B. BRADY, Roy Meredith. Over 300 Brady photos reproduced directly from original negatives, photos. Lively commentary. 368pp. 8⅜ × 11¼. 23021-X Pa. $11.95

PHOTOGRAPHIC VIEWS OF SHERMAN'S CAMPAIGN, George N. Barnard. Reprint of landmark 1866 volume with 61 plates: battlefield of New Hope Church, the Etawah Bridge, the capture of Atlanta, etc. 80pp. 9 × 12. 23445-2 Pa. $6.00

A SHORT HISTORY OF ANATOMY AND PHYSIOLOGY FROM THE GREEKS TO HARVEY, Dr. Charles Singer. Thoroughly engrossing non-technical survey. 270 illustrations. 211pp. 5⅜ × 8½. 20389-1 Pa. $4.50

REDOUTE ROSES IRON-ON TRANSFER PATTERNS, Barbara Christopher. Redouté was botanical painter to the Empress Josephine; transfer his famous roses onto fabric with these 24 transfer patterns. 80pp. 8¼ × 10⅞. 24292-7 Pa. $3.50

THE FIVE BOOKS OF ARCHITECTURE, Sebastiano Serlio. Architectural milestone, first (1611) English translation of Renaissance classic. Unabridged reproduction of original edition includes over 300 woodcut illustrations. 416pp. 9⅜ × 12¼. 24349-4 Pa. $14.95

CARLSON'S GUIDE TO LANDSCAPE PAINTING, John F. Carlson. Authoritative, comprehensive guide covers, every aspect of landscape painting. 34 reproductions of paintings by author; 58 explanatory diagrams. 144pp. 8⅜ × 11. 22927-0 Pa. $4.95

101 PUZZLES IN THOUGHT AND LOGIC, C.R. Wylie, Jr. Solve murders, robberies, see which fishermen are liars—purely by reasoning! 107pp. 5⅜ × 8½. 20367-0 Pa. $2.00

TEST YOUR LOGIC, George J. Summers. 50 more truly new puzzles with new turns of thought, new subtleties of inference. 100pp. 5⅜ × 8½. 22877-0 Pa. $2.25

THE MURDER BOOK OF J.G. REEDER, Edgar Wallace. Eight suspenseful stories by bestselling mystery writer of 20s and 30s. Features the donnish Mr. J.G. Reeder of Public Prosecutor's Office. 128pp. 5⅜ × 8½. (Available in U.S. only)
24374-5 Pa. $3.50

ANNE ORR'S CHARTED DESIGNS, Anne Orr. Best designs by premier needlework designer, all on charts: flowers, borders, birds, children, alphabets, etc. Over 100 charts, 10 in color. Total of 40pp. 8¼ × 11.
23704-4 Pa. $2.25

BASIC CONSTRUCTION TECHNIQUES FOR HOUSES AND SMALL BUILDINGS SIMPLY EXPLAINED, U.S. Bureau of Naval Personnel. Grading, masonry, woodworking, floor and wall framing, roof framing, plastering, tile setting, much more. Over 675 illustrations. 568pp. 6½ × 9¼.
20242-9 Pa. $8.95

MATISSE LINE DRAWINGS AND PRINTS, Henri Matisse. Representative collection of female nudes, faces, still lifes, experimental works, etc., from 1898 to 1948. 50 illustrations. 48pp. 8⅜ × 11¼.
23877-6 Pa. $2.50

HOW TO PLAY THE CHESS OPENINGS, Eugene Znosko-Borovsky. Clear, profound examinations of just what each opening is intended to do and how opponent can counter. Many sample games. 147pp. 5⅜ × 8½.
22795-2 Pa. $2.95

DUPLICATE BRIDGE, Alfred Sheinwold. Clear, thorough, easily followed account: rules, etiquette, scoring, strategy, bidding; Goren's point-count system, Blackwood and Gerber conventions, etc. 158pp. 5⅜ × 8½.
22741-3 Pa. $3.00

SARGENT PORTRAIT DRAWINGS, J.S. Sargent. Collection of 42 portraits reveals technical skill and intuitive eye of noted American portrait painter, John Singer Sargent. 48pp. 8¼ × 11⅛.
24524-1 Pa. $2.95

ENTERTAINING SCIENCE EXPERIMENTS WITH EVERYDAY OBJECTS, Martin Gardner. Over 100 experiments for youngsters. Will amuse, astonish, teach, and entertain. Over 100 illustrations. 127pp. 5⅜ × 8½.
24201-3 Pa. $2.50

TEDDY BEAR PAPER DOLLS IN FULL COLOR: A Family of Four Bears and Their Costumes, Crystal Collins. A family of four Teddy Bear paper dolls and nearly 60 cut-out costumes. Full color, printed one side only. 32pp. 9¼ × 12¼.
24550-0 Pa. $3.50

NEW CALLIGRAPHIC ORNAMENTS AND FLOURISHES, Arthur Baker. Unusual, multi-useable material: arrows, pointing hands, brackets and frames, ovals, swirls, birds, etc. Nearly 700 illustrations. 80pp. 8⅜ × 11¼.
24095-9 Pa. $3.75

DINOSAUR DIORAMAS TO CUT & ASSEMBLE, M. Kalmenoff. Two complete three-dimensional scenes in full color, with 31 cut-out animals and plants. Excellent educational toy for youngsters. Instructions; 2 assembly diagrams. 32pp. 9¼ × 12¼.
24541-1 Pa. $3.95

SILHOUETTES: A PICTORIAL ARCHIVE OF VARIED ILLUSTRATIONS, edited by Carol Belanger Grafton. Over 600 silhouettes from the 18th to 20th centuries. Profiles and full figures of men, women, children, birds, animals, groups and scenes, nature, ships, an alphabet. 144pp. 8⅜ × 11¼.
23781-8 Pa. $4.95

25 KITES THAT FLY, Leslie Hunt. Full, easy-to-follow instructions for kites made from inexpensive materials. Many novelties. 70 illustrations. 110pp. 5⅜ × 8½.
22550-X Pa. $2.25

PIANO TUNING, J. Cree Fischer. Clearest, best book for beginner, amateur. Simple repairs, raising dropped notes, tuning by easy method of flattened fifths. No previous skills needed. 4 illustrations. 201pp. 5⅜ × 8½. 23267-0 Pa. $3.50

EARLY AMERICAN IRON-ON TRANSFER PATTERNS, edited by Rita Weiss. 75 designs, borders, alphabets, from traditional American sources. 48pp. 8¼ × 11.
23162-3 Pa. $1.95

CROCHETING EDGINGS, edited by Rita Weiss. Over 100 of the best designs for these lovely trims for a host of household items. Complete instructions, illustrations. 48pp. 8¼ × 11. 24031-2 Pa. $2.25

FINGER PLAYS FOR NURSERY AND KINDERGARTEN, Emilie Poulsson. 18 finger plays with music (voice and piano); entertaining, instructive. Counting, nature lore, etc. Victorian classic. 53 illustrations. 80pp. 6½ × 9¼. 22588-7 Pa. $1.95

BOSTON THEN AND NOW, Peter Vanderwarker. Here in 59 side-by-side views are photographic documentations of the city's past and present. 119 photographs. Full captions. 122pp. 8¼ × 11. 24312-5 Pa. $6.95

CROCHETING BEDSPREADS, edited by Rita Weiss. 22 patterns, originally published in three instruction books 1939-41. 39 photos, 8 charts. Instructions. 48pp. 8¼ × 11. 23610-2 Pa. $2.00

HAWTHORNE ON PAINTING, Charles W. Hawthorne. Collected from notes taken by students at famous Cape Cod School; hundreds of direct, personal *apercus*, ideas, suggestions. 91pp. 5⅜ × 8½. 20653-X Pa. $2.50

THERMODYNAMICS, Enrico Fermi. A classic of modern science. Clear, organized treatment of systems, first and second laws, entropy, thermodynamic potentials, etc. Calculus required. 160pp. 5⅜ × 8½. 60361-X Pa. $4.00

TEN BOOKS ON ARCHITECTURE, Vitruvius. The most important book ever written on architecture. Early Roman aesthetics, technology, classical orders, site selection, all other aspects. Morgan translation. 331pp. 5⅜ × 8½. 20645-9 Pa. $5.50

THE CORNELL BREAD BOOK, Clive M. McCay and Jeanette B. McCay. Famed high-protein recipe incorporated into breads, rolls, buns, coffee cakes, pizza, pie crusts, more. Nearly 50 illustrations. 48pp. 8¼ × 11. 23995-0 Pa. $2.00

THE CRAFTSMAN'S HANDBOOK, Cennino Cennini. 15th-century handbook, school of Giotto, explains applying gold, silver leaf; gesso; fresco painting, grinding pigments, etc. 142pp. 6⅛ × 9¼. 20054-X Pa. $3.50

FRANK LLOYD WRIGHT'S FALLINGWATER, Donald Hoffmann. Full story of Wright's masterwork at Bear Run, Pa. 100 photographs of site, construction, and details of completed structure. 112pp. 9¼ × 10. 23671-4 Pa. $6.50

OVAL STAINED GLASS PATTERN BOOK, C. Eaton. 60 new designs framed in shape of an oval. Greater complexity, challenge with sinuous cats, birds, mandalas framed in antique shape. 64pp. 8¼ × 11. 24519-5 Pa. $3.50

THE BOOK OF WOOD CARVING, Charles Marshall Sayers. Still finest book for beginning student. Fundamentals, technique; gives 34 designs, over 34 projects for panels, bookends, mirrors, etc. 33 photos. 118pp. 7¾ × 10⅝. 23654-4 Pa. $3.95

CARVING COUNTRY CHARACTERS, Bill Higginbotham. Expert advice for beginning, advanced carvers on materials, techniques for creating 18 projects— mirthful panorama of American characters. 105 illustrations. 80pp. 8⅜ × 11. 24135-1 Pa. $2.50

300 ART NOUVEAU DESIGNS AND MOTIFS IN FULL COLOR, C.B. Grafton. 44 full-page plates display swirling lines and muted colors typical of Art Nouveau. Borders, frames, panels, cartouches, dingbats, etc. 48pp. 9⅜ × 12¼. 24354-0 Pa. $6.00

SELF-WORKING CARD TRICKS, Karl Fulves. Editor of *Pallbearer* offers 72 tricks that work automatically through nature of card deck. No sleight of hand needed. Often spectacular. 42 illustrations. 113pp. 5⅜ × 8½. 23334-0 Pa. $3.50

CUT AND ASSEMBLE A WESTERN FRONTIER TOWN, Edmund V. Gillon, Jr. Ten authentic full-color buildings on heavy cardboard stock in H-O scale. Sheriff's Office and Jail, Saloon, Wells Fargo, Opera House, others. 48pp. 9¼ × 12¼. 23736-2 Pa. $3.95

CUT AND ASSEMBLE AN EARLY NEW ENGLAND VILLAGE, Edmund V. Gillon, Jr. Printed in full color on heavy cardboard stock. 12 authentic buildings in H-O scale: Adams home in Quincy, Mass., Oliver Wight house in Sturbridge, smithy, store, church, others. 48pp. 9¼ × 12¼. 23536-X Pa. $3.95

THE TALE OF TWO BAD MICE, Beatrix Potter. Tom Thumb and Hunca Munca squeeze out of their hole and go exploring. 27 full-color Potter illustrations. 59pp. 4¼ × 5½. (Available in U.S. only) 23065-1 Pa. $1.50

CARVING FIGURE CARICATURES IN THE OZARK STYLE, Harold L. Enlow. Instructions and illustrations for ten delightful projects, plus general carving instructions. 22 drawings and 47 photographs altogether. 39pp. 8⅜ × 11. 23151-8 Pa. $2.50

A TREASURY OF FLOWER DESIGNS FOR ARTISTS, EMBROIDERERS AND CRAFTSMEN, Susan Gaber. 100 garden favorites lushly rendered by artist for artists, craftsmen, needleworkers. Many form frames, borders. 80pp. 8¼ × 11. 24096-7 Pa. $3.50

CUT & ASSEMBLE A TOY THEATER/THE NUTCRACKER BALLET, Tom Tierney. Model of a complete, full-color production of Tchaikovsky's classic. 6 backdrops, dozens of characters, familiar dance sequences. 32pp. 9⅜ × 12¼. 24194-7 Pa. $4.50

ANIMALS: 1,419 COPYRIGHT-FREE ILLUSTRATIONS OF MAMMALS, BIRDS, FISH, INSECTS, ETC., edited by Jim Harter. Clear wood engravings present, in extremely lifelike poses, over 1,000 species of animals. 284pp. 9 × 12. 23766-4 Pa. $9.95

MORE HAND SHADOWS, Henry Bursill. For those at their 'finger ends," 16 more effects—Shakespeare, a hare, a squirrel, Mr. Punch, and twelve more—each explained by a full-page illustration. Considerable period charm. 30pp. 6½ × 9¼. 21384-6 Pa. $1.95

CATALOG OF DOVER BOOKS

SURREAL STICKERS AND UNREAL STAMPS, William Rowe. 224 haunting, hilarious stamps on gummed, perforated stock, with images of elephants, geisha girls, George Washington, etc. 16pp. one side. 8¼ × 11.   24371-0 Pa. $3.50

GOURMET KITCHEN LABELS, Ed Sibbett, Jr. 112 full-color labels (4 copies each of 28 designs). Fruit, bread, other culinary motifs. Gummed and perforated. 16pp. 8¼ × 11.   24087-8 Pa. $2.95

PATTERNS AND INSTRUCTIONS FOR CARVING AUTHENTIC BIRDS, H.D. Green. Detailed instructions, 27 diagrams, 85 photographs for carving 15 species of birds so life-like, they'll seem ready to fly! 8¼ × 11.   24222-6 Pa. $2.75

FLATLAND, E.A. Abbott. Science-fiction classic explores life of 2-D being in 3-D world. 16 illustrations. 103pp. 5⅜ × 8.   20001-9 Pa. $2.00

DRIED FLOWERS, Sarah Whitlock and Martha Rankin. Concise, clear, practical guide to dehydration, glycerinizing, pressing plant material, and more. Covers use of silica gel. 12 drawings. 32pp. 5⅜ × 8½.   21802-3 Pa. $1.00

EASY-TO-MAKE CANDLES, Gary V. Guy. Learn how easy it is to make all kinds of decorative candles. Step-by-step instructions. 82 illustrations. 48pp. 8¼ × 11.
          23881-4 Pa. $2.50

SUPER STICKERS FOR KIDS, Carolyn Bracken. 128 gummed and perforated full-color stickers: GIRL WANTED, KEEP OUT, BORED OF EDUCATION, X-RATED, COMBAT ZONE, many others. 16pp. 8¼ × 11.   24092-4 Pa. $2.50

CUT AND COLOR PAPER MASKS, Michael Grater. Clowns, animals, funny faces...simply color them in, cut them out, and put them together, and you have 9 paper masks to play with and enjoy. 32pp. 8¼ × 11.   23171-2 Pa. $2.25

A CHRISTMAS CAROL: THE ORIGINAL MANUSCRIPT, Charles Dickens. Clear facsimile of Dickens manuscript, on facing pages with final printed text. 8 illustrations by John Leech, 4 in color on covers. 144pp. 8⅜ × 11¼.
          20980-6 Pa. $5.95

CARVING SHOREBIRDS, Harry V. Shourds & Anthony Hillman. 16 full-size patterns (all double-page spreads) for 19 North American shorebirds with step-by-step instructions. 72pp. 9¼ × 12¼.   24287-0 Pa. $4.95

THE GENTLE ART OF MATHEMATICS, Dan Pedoe. Mathematical games, probability, the question of infinity, topology, how the laws of algebra work, problems of irrational numbers, and more. 42 figures. 143pp. 5⅜ × 8½. (EBE)
          22949-1 Pa. $3.50

READY-TO-USE DOLLHOUSE WALLPAPER, Katzenbach & Warren, Inc. Stripe, 2 floral stripes, 2 allover florals, polka dot; all in full color. 4 sheets (350 sq. in.) of each, enough for average room. 48pp. 8¼ × 11.   23495-9 Pa. $2.95

MINIATURE IRON-ON TRANSFER PATTERNS FOR DOLLHOUSES, DOLLS, AND SMALL PROJECTS, Rita Weiss and Frank Fontana. Over 100 miniature patterns: rugs, bedspreads, quilts, chair seats, etc. In standard dollhouse size. 48pp. 8¼ × 11.   23741-9 Pa. $1.95

THE DINOSAUR COLORING BOOK, Anthony Rao. 45 renderings of dinosaurs, fossil birds, turtles, other creatures of Mesozoic Era. Scientifically accurate. Captions. 48pp. 8¼ × 11.   24022-3 Pa. $2.25

JAPANESE DESIGN MOTIFS, Matsuya Co. Mon, or heraldic designs. Over 4000 typical, beautiful designs: birds, animals, flowers, swords, fans, geometrics; all beautifully stylized. 213pp. 11⅜ × 8¼. 22874-6 Pa. $7.95

THE TALE OF BENJAMIN BUNNY, Beatrix Potter. Peter Rabbit's cousin coaxes him back into Mr. McGregor's garden for a whole new set of adventures. All 27 full-color illustrations. 59pp. 4¼ × 5½. (Available in U.S. only) 21102-9 Pa. $1.50

THE TALE OF PETER RABBIT AND OTHER FAVORITE STORIES BOXED SET, Beatrix Potter. Seven of Beatrix Potter's best-loved tales including Peter Rabbit in a specially designed, durable boxed set. 4¼ × 5½. Total of 447pp. 158 color illustrations. (Available in U.S. only) 23903-9 Pa. $10.80

PRACTICAL MENTAL MAGIC, Theodore Annemann. Nearly 200 astonishing feats of mental magic revealed in step-by-step detail. Complete advice on staging, patter, etc. Illustrated. 320pp. 5⅜ × 8½. 24426-1 Pa. $5.95

CELEBRATED CASES OF JUDGE DEE (DEE GOONG AN), translated by Robert Van Gulik. Authentic 18th-century Chinese detective novel; Dee and associates solve three interlocked cases. Led to van Gulik's own stories with same characters. Extensive introduction. 9 illustrations. 237pp. 5⅜ × 8½. 23337-5 Pa. $4.50

CUT & FOLD EXTRATERRESTRIAL INVADERS THAT FLY, M. Grater. Stage your own lilliputian space battles.By following the step-by-step instructions and explanatory diagrams you can launch 22 full-color fliers into space. 36pp. 8¼ × 11. 24478-4 Pa. $2.95

CUT & ASSEMBLE VICTORIAN HOUSES, Edmund V. Gillon, Jr. Printed in full color on heavy cardboard stock, 4 authentic Victorian houses in H-O scale: Italian-style Villa, Octagon, Second Empire, Stick Style. 48pp. 9¼ × 12¼. 23849-0 Pa. $3.95

BEST SCIENCE FICTION STORIES OF H.G. WELLS, H.G. Wells. Full novel *The Invisible Man,* plus 17 short stories: "The Crystal Egg," "Aepyornis Island," "The Strange Orchid," etc. 303pp. 5⅜ × 8½. (Available in U.S. only) 21531-8 Pa. $4.95

TRADEMARK DESIGNS OF THE WORLD, Yusaku Kamekura. A lavish collection of nearly 700 trademarks, the work of Wright, Loewy, Klee, Binder, hundreds of others. 160pp. 8¾ × 8. (Available in U.S. only) 24191-2 Pa. $5.00

THE ARTIST'S AND CRAFTSMAN'S GUIDE TO REDUCING, ENLARGING AND TRANSFERRING DESIGNS, Rita Weiss. Discover, reduce, enlarge, transfer designs from any objects to any craft project. 12pp. plus 16 sheets special graph paper. 8¼ × 11. 24142-4 Pa. $3.25

TREASURY OF JAPANESE DESIGNS AND MOTIFS FOR ARTISTS AND CRAFTSMEN, edited by Carol Belanger Grafton. Indispensable collection of 360 traditional Japanese designs and motifs redrawn in clean, crisp black-and-white, copyright-free illustrations. 96pp. 8¼ × 11. 24435-0 Pa. $3.95

CHANCERY CURSIVE STROKE BY STROKE, Arthur Baker. Instructions and illustrations for each stroke of each letter (upper and lower case) and numerals. 54 full-page plates. 64pp. 8¼ × 11.　　　　　　　　　　　　　　24278-1 Pa. $2.50

THE ENJOYMENT AND USE OF COLOR, Walter Sargent. Color relationships, values, intensities; complementary colors, illumination, similar topics. Color in nature and art. 7 color plates, 29 illustrations. 274pp. 5⅜ × 8½.　　20944-X Pa. $4.50

SCULPTURE PRINCIPLES AND PRACTICE, Louis Slobodkin. Step-by-step approach to clay, plaster, metals, stone; classical and modern. 253 drawings, photos. 255pp. 8⅛ × 11.　　　　　　　　　　　　　　　22960-2 Pa. $7.50

VICTORIAN FASHION PAPER DOLLS FROM HARPER'S BAZAR, 1867-1898, Theodore Menten. Four female dolls with 28 elegant high fashion costumes, printed in full color. 32pp. 9¼ × 12¼.　　　　　　　　　　23453-3 Pa. $3.50

FLOPSY, MOPSY AND COTTONTAIL: A Little Book of Paper Dolls in Full Color, Susan LaBelle. Three dolls and 21 costumes (7 for each doll) show Peter Rabbit's siblings dressed for holidays, gardening, hiking, etc. Charming borders, captions. 48pp. 4¼ × 5½.　　　　　　　　　　　　　　24376-1 Pa. $2.25

NATIONAL LEAGUE BASEBALL CARD CLASSICS, Bert Randolph Sugar. 83 big-leaguers from 1909-69 on facsimile cards. Hubbell, Dean, Spahn, Brock plus advertising, info, no duplications. Perforated, detachable. 16pp. 8¼ × 11.
　　　　　　　　　　　　　　　　　　　　　　　　24308-7 Pa. $2.95

THE LOGICAL APPROACH TO CHESS, Dr. Max Euwe, et al. First-rate text of comprehensive strategy, tactics, theory for the amateur. No gambits to memorize, just a clear, logical approach. 224pp. 5⅜ × 8½.　　　　　　24353-2 Pa. $4.50

MAGICK IN THEORY AND PRACTICE, Aleister Crowley. The summation of the thought and practice of the century's most famous necromancer, long hard to find. Crowley's best book. 436pp. 5⅜ × 8½. (Available in U.S. only)
　　　　　　　　　　　　　　　　　　　　　　　　23295-6 Pa. $6.50

THE HAUNTED HOTEL, Wilkie Collins. Collins' last great tale; doom and destiny in a Venetian palace. Praised by T.S. Eliot. 127pp. 5⅜ × 8½.
　　　　　　　　　　　　　　　　　　　　　　　　24333-8 Pa. $3.00

ART DECO DISPLAY ALPHABETS, Dan X. Solo. Wide variety of bold yet elegant lettering in handsome Art Deco styles. 100 complete fonts, with numerals, punctuation, more. 104pp. 8⅛ × 11.　　　　　　　　　　　24372-9 Pa. $4.00

CALLIGRAPHIC ALPHABETS, Arthur Baker. Nearly 150 complete alphabets by outstanding contemporary. Stimulating ideas; useful source for unique effects. 154 plates. 157pp. 8⅜ × 11¼.　　　　　　　　　　　　　　21045-6 Pa. $4.95

ARTHUR BAKER'S HISTORIC CALLIGRAPHIC ALPHABETS, Arthur Baker. From monumental capitals of first-century Rome to humanistic cursive of 16th century, 33 alphabets in fresh interpretations. 88 plates. 96pp. 9 × 12.
　　　　　　　　　　　　　　　　　　　　　　　　24054-1 Pa. $4.50

LETTIE LANE PAPER DOLLS, Sheila Young. Genteel turn-of-the-century family very popular then and now. 24 paper dolls. 16 plates in full color. 32pp. 9¼ × 12¼.　　　　　　　　　　　　　　　　　　　　24089-4 Pa. $3.50

KEYBOARD WORKS FOR SOLO INSTRUMENTS, G.F. Handel. 35 neglected works from Handel's vast oeuvre, originally jotted down as improvisations. Includes Eight Great Suites, others. New sequence. 174pp. 9⅜ × 12¼.
24338-9 Pa. $7.50

AMERICAN LEAGUE BASEBALL CARD CLASSICS, Bert Randolph Sugar. 82 stars from 1900s to 60s on facsimile cards. Ruth, Cobb, Mantle, Williams, plus advertising, info, no duplications. Perforated, detachable. 16pp. 8¼ × 11.
24286-2 Pa. $2.95

A TREASURY OF CHARTED DESIGNS FOR NEEDLEWORKERS, Georgia Gorham and Jeanne Warth. 141 charted designs: owl, cat with yarn, tulips, piano, spinning wheel, covered bridge, Victorian house and many others. 48pp. 8¼ × 11.
23558-0 Pa. $1.95

DANISH FLORAL CHARTED DESIGNS, Gerda Bengtsson. Exquisite collection of over 40 different florals: anemone, Iceland poppy, wild fruit, pansies, many others. 45 illustrations. 48pp. 8¼ × 11.
23957-8 Pa. $1.75

OLD PHILADELPHIA IN EARLY PHOTOGRAPHS 1839-1914, Robert F. Looney. 215 photographs: panoramas, street scenes, landmarks, President-elect Lincoln's visit, 1876 Centennial Exposition, much more. 230pp. 8⅜ × 11¾.
23345-6 Pa. $9.95

PRELUDE TO MATHEMATICS, W.W. Sawyer. Noted mathematician's lively, stimulating account of non-Euclidean geometry, matrices, determinants, group theory, other topics. Emphasis on novel, striking aspects. 224pp. 5⅜ × 8½.
24401-6 Pa. $4.50

ADVENTURES WITH A MICROSCOPE, Richard Headstrom. 59 adventures with clothing fibers, protozoa, ferns and lichens, roots and leaves, much more. 142 illustrations. 232pp. 5⅜ × 8½.
23471-1 Pa. $3.95

IDENTIFYING ANIMAL TRACKS: MAMMALS, BIRDS, AND OTHER ANIMALS OF THE EASTERN UNITED STATES, Richard Headstrom. For hunters, naturalists, scouts, nature-lovers. Diagrams of tracks, tips on identification. 128pp. 5⅜ × 8.
24442-3 Pa. $3.50

VICTORIAN FASHIONS AND COSTUMES FROM HARPER'S BAZAR, 1867-1898, edited by Stella Blum. Day costumes, evening wear, sports clothes, shoes, hats, other accessories in over 1,000 detailed engravings. 320pp. 9⅜ × 12¼.
22990-4 Pa. $9.95

EVERYDAY FASHIONS OF THE TWENTIES AS PICTURED IN SEARS AND OTHER CATALOGS, edited by Stella Blum. Actual dress of the Roaring Twenties, with text by Stella Blum. Over 750 illustrations, captions. 156pp. 9 × 12.
24134-3 Pa. $8.50

HALL OF FAME BASEBALL CARDS, edited by Bert Randolph Sugar. Cy Young, Ted Williams, Lou Gehrig, and many other Hall of Fame greats on 92 full-color, detachable reprints of early baseball cards. No duplication of cards with *Classic Baseball Cards*. 16pp. 8¼ × 11.
23624-2 Pa. $3.50

THE ART OF HAND LETTERING, Helm Wotzkow. Course in hand lettering, Roman, Gothic, Italic, Block, Script. Tools, proportions, optical aspects, individual variation. Very quality conscious. Hundreds of specimens. 320pp. 5⅜ × 8½.
21797-3 Pa. $4.95

HOW THE OTHER HALF LIVES, Jacob A. Riis. Journalistic record of filth, degradation, upward drive in New York immigrant slums, shops, around 1900. New edition includes 100 original Riis photos, monuments of early photography. 233pp. 10 × 7⅞.   22012-5 Pa. $7.95

CHINA AND ITS PEOPLE IN EARLY PHOTOGRAPHS, John Thomson. In 200 black-and-white photographs of exceptional quality photographic pioneer Thomson captures the mountains, dwellings, monuments and people of 19th-century China. 272pp. 9⅜ × 12¼.   24393-1 Pa. $12.95

GODEY COSTUME PLATES IN COLOR FOR DECOUPAGE AND FRAMING, edited by Eleanor Hasbrouk Rawlings. 24 full-color engravings depicting 19th-century Parisian haute couture. Printed on one side only. 56pp. 8¼ × 11.   23879-2 Pa. $3.95

ART NOUVEAU STAINED GLASS PATTERN BOOK, Ed Sibbett, Jr. 104 projects using well-known themes of Art Nouveau: swirling forms, florals, peacocks, and sensuous women. 60pp. 8¼ × 11.   23577-7 Pa. $3.50

QUICK AND EASY PATCHWORK ON THE SEWING MACHINE: Susan Aylsworth Murwin and Suzzy Payne. Instructions, diagrams show exactly how to machine sew 12 quilts. 48pp. of templates. 50 figures. 80pp. 8¼ × 11.   23770-2 Pa. $3.50

THE STANDARD BOOK OF QUILT MAKING AND COLLECTING, Marguerite Ickis. Full information, full-sized patterns for making 46 traditional quilts, also 150 other patterns. 483 illustrations. 273pp. 6⅞ × 9⅝. 20582-7 Pa. $5.95

LETTERING AND ALPHABETS, J. Albert Cavanagh. 85 complete alphabets lettered in various styles; instructions for spacing, roughs, brushwork. 121pp. 8¾ × 8.   20053-1 Pa. $3.75

LETTER FORMS: 110 COMPLETE ALPHABETS, Frederick Lambert. 110 sets of capital letters; 16 lower case alphabets; 70 sets of numbers and other symbols. 110pp. 8⅛ × 11.   22872-X Pa. $4.50

ORCHIDS AS HOUSE PLANTS, Rebecca Tyson Northen. Grow cattleyas and many other kinds of orchids—in a window, in a case, or under artificial light. 63 illustrations. 148pp. 5⅜ × 8½.   23261-1 Pa. $2.95

THE MUSHROOM HANDBOOK, Louis C.C. Krieger. Still the best popular handbook. Full descriptions of 259 species, extremely thorough text, poisons, folklore, etc. 32 color plates; 126 other illustrations. 560pp. 5⅜ × 8½.   21861-9 Pa. $8.50

THE DORÉ BIBLE ILLUSTRATIONS, Gustave Doré. All wonderful, detailed plates: Adam and Eve, Flood, Babylon, life of Jesus, etc. Brief King James text with each plate. 241 plates. 241pp. 9 × 12.   23004-X Pa. $8.95

THE BOOK OF KELLS: Selected Plates in Full Color, edited by Blanche Cirker. 32 full-page plates from greatest manuscript-icon of early Middle Ages. Fantastic, mysterious. Publisher's Note. Captions. 32pp. 9¾ × 12¼.   24345-1 Pa. $4.50

THE PERFECT WAGNERITE, George Bernard Shaw. Brilliant criticism of the Ring Cycle, with provocative interpretation of politics, economic theories behind the Ring. 136pp. 5⅜ × 8½. (Available in U.S. only)   21707-8 Pa. $3.00

THE RIME OF THE ANCIENT MARINER, Gustave Doré, S.T. Coleridge. Doré's finest work, 34 plates capture moods, subtleties of poem. Full text. 77pp. 9¼ × 12. 22305-1 Pa. $4.95

SONGS OF INNOCENCE, William Blake. The first and most popular of Blake's famous "Illuminated Books," in a facsimile edition reproducing all 31 brightly colored plates. Additional printed text of each poem. 64pp. 5¼ × 7. 22764-2 Pa. $3.00

AN INTRODUCTION TO INFORMATION THEORY, J.R. Pierce. Second (1980) edition of most impressive non-technical account available. Encoding, entropy, noisy channel, related areas, etc. 320pp. 5⅜ × 8½. 24061-4 Pa. $4.95

THE DIVINE PROPORTION: A STUDY IN MATHEMATICAL BEAUTY, H.E. Huntley. "Divine proportion" or "golden ratio" in poetry, Pascal's triangle, philosophy, psychology, music, mathematical figures, etc. Excellent bridge between science and art. 58 figures. 185pp. 5⅜ × 8½. 22254-3 Pa. $3.95

THE DOVER NEW YORK WALKING GUIDE: From the Battery to Wall Street, Mary J. Shapiro. Superb inexpensive guide to historic buildings and locales in lower Manhattan: Trinity Church, Bowling Green, more. Complete Text; maps. 36 illustrations. 48pp. 3⅞ × 9¼. 24225-0 Pa. $2.50

NEW YORK THEN AND NOW, Edward B. Watson, Edmund V. Gillon, Jr. 83 important Manhattan sites: on facing pages early photographs (1875-1925) and 1976 photos by Gillon. 172 illustrations. 171pp. 9¼ × 10. 23361-8 Pa. $7.95

HISTORIC COSTUME IN PICTURES, Braun & Schneider. Over 1450 costumed figures from dawn of civilization to end of 19th century. English captions. 125 plates. 256pp. 8⅜ × 11¼. 23150-X Pa. $7.50

VICTORIAN AND EDWARDIAN FASHION: A Photographic Survey, Alison Gernsheim. First fashion history completely illustrated by contemporary photographs. Full text plus 235 photos, 1840-1914, in which many celebrities appear. 240pp. 6½ × 9¼. 24205-6 Pa. $6.00

CHARTED CHRISTMAS DESIGNS FOR COUNTED CROSS-STITCH AND OTHER NEEDLECRAFTS, Lindberg Press. Charted designs for 45 beautiful needlecraft projects with many yuletide and wintertime motifs. 48pp. 8¼ × 11. 24356-7 Pa. $1.95

101 FOLK DESIGNS FOR COUNTED CROSS-STITCH AND OTHER NEEDLECRAFTS, Carter Houck. 101 authentic charted folk designs in a wide array of lovely representations with many suggestions for effective use. 48pp. 8¼ × 11. 24369-9 Pa. $2.25

FIVE ACRES AND INDEPENDENCE, Maurice G. Kains. Great back-to-the-land classic explains basics of self-sufficient farming. The one book to get. 95 illustrations. 397pp. 5⅜ × 8½. 20974-1 Pa. $4.95

A MODERN HERBAL, Margaret Grieve. Much the fullest, most exact, most useful compilation of herbal material. Gigantic alphabetical encyclopedia, from aconite to zedoary, gives botanical information, medical properties, folklore, economic uses, and much else. Indispensable to serious reader. 161 illustrations. 888pp. 6½ × 9¼. (Available in U.S. only) 22798-7, 22799-5 Pa., Two-vol. set $16.45

DECORATIVE NAPKIN FOLDING FOR BEGINNERS, Lillian Oppenheimer and Natalie Epstein. 22 different napkin folds in the shape of a heart, clown's hat, love knot, etc. 63 drawings. 48pp. 8¼ × 11. 23797-4 Pa. $1.95

DECORATIVE LABELS FOR HOME CANNING, PRESERVING, AND OTHER HOUSEHOLD AND GIFT USES, Theodore Menten. 128 gummed, perforated labels, beautifully printed in 2 colors. 12 versions. Adhere to metal, glass, wood, ceramics. 24pp. 8¼ × 11. 23219-0 Pa. $2.95

EARLY AMERICAN STENCILS ON WALLS AND FURNITURE, Janet Waring. Thorough coverage of 19th-century folk art: techniques, artifacts, surviving specimens. 166 illustrations, 7 in color. 147pp. of text. 7⅞ × 10¾. 21906-2 Pa. $9.95

AMERICAN ANTIQUE WEATHERVANES, A.B. & W.T. Westervelt. Extensively illustrated 1883 catalog exhibiting over 550 copper weathervanes and finials. Excellent primary source by one of the principal manufacturers. 104pp. 6⅛ × 9¼. 24396-6 Pa. $3.95

ART STUDENTS' ANATOMY, Edmond J. Farris. Long favorite in art schools. Basic elements, common positions, actions. Full text, 158 illustrations. 159pp. 5⅜ × 8½. 20744-7 Pa. $3.95

BRIDGMAN'S LIFE DRAWING, George B. Bridgman. More than 500 drawings and text teach you to abstract the body into its major masses. Also specific areas of anatomy. 192pp. 6½ × 9¼. (EA) 22710-3 Pa. $4.50

COMPLETE PRELUDES AND ETUDES FOR SOLO PIANO, Frederic Chopin. All 26 Preludes, all 27 Etudes by greatest composer of piano music. Authoritative Paderewski edition. 224pp. 9 × 12. (Available in U.S. only) 24052-5 Pa. $7.50

PIANO MUSIC 1888-1905, Claude Debussy. Deux Arabesques, Suite Bergamesque, Masques, 1st series of Images, etc. 9 others, in corrected editions. 175pp. 9⅜ × 12¼. (ECE) 22771-5 Pa. $5.95

TEDDY BEAR IRON-ON TRANSFER PATTERNS, Ted Menten. 80 iron-on transfer patterns of male and female Teddys in a wide variety of activities, poses, sizes. 48pp. 8¼ × 11. 24596-9 Pa. $2.25

A PICTURE HISTORY OF THE BROOKLYN BRIDGE, M.J. Shapiro. Profusely illustrated account of greatest engineering achievement of 19th century. 167 rare photos & engravings recall construction, human drama. Extensive, detailed text. 122pp. 8¼ × 11. 24403-2 Pa. $7.95

NEW YORK IN THE THIRTIES, Berenice Abbott. Noted photographer's fascinating study shows new buildings that have become famous and old sights that have disappeared forever. 97 photographs. 97pp. 11⅜ × 10. 22967-X Pa. $6.50

MATHEMATICAL TABLES AND FORMULAS, Robert D. Carmichael and Edwin R. Smith. Logarithms, sines, tangents, trig functions, powers, roots, reciprocals, exponential and hyperbolic functions, formulas and theorems. 269pp. 5⅜ × 8½. 60111-0 Pa. $3.75

HANDBOOK OF MATHEMATICAL FUNCTIONS WITH FORMULAS, GRAPHS, AND MATHEMATICAL TABLES, edited by Milton Abramowitz and Irene A. Stegun. Vast compendium: 29 sets of tables, some to as high as 20 places. 1,046pp. 8 × 10½. 61272-4 Pa. $19.95

REASON IN ART, George Santayana. Renowned philosopher's provocative, seminal treatment of basis of art in instinct and experience. Volume Four of *The Life of Reason*. 230pp. 5⅜ × 8.   24358-3 Pa. $4.50

LANGUAGE, TRUTH AND LOGIC, Alfred J. Ayer. Famous, clear introduction to Vienna, Cambridge schools of Logical Positivism. Role of philosophy, elimination of metaphysics, nature of analysis, etc. 160pp. 5⅜ × 8½. (USCO)
20010-8 Pa. $2.75

BASIC ELECTRONICS, U.S. Bureau of Naval Personnel. Electron tubes, circuits, antennas, AM, FM, and CW transmission and receiving, etc. 560 illustrations. 567pp. 6½ × 9¼.   21076-6 Pa. $8.95

THE ART DECO STYLE, edited by Theodore Menten. Furniture, jewelry, metalwork, ceramics, fabrics, lighting fixtures, interior decors, exteriors, graphics from pure French sources. Over 400 photographs. 183pp. 8⅜ × 11¼.
22824-X Pa. $6.95

THE FOUR BOOKS OF ARCHITECTURE, Andrea Palladio. 16th-century classic covers classical architectural remains, Renaissance revivals, classical orders, etc. 1738 Ware English edition. 216 plates. 110pp. of text. 9½ × 12¾.
21308-0 Pa. $11.50

THE WIT AND HUMOR OF OSCAR WILDE, edited by Alvin Redman. More than 1000 ripostes, paradoxes, wisecracks: Work is the curse of the drinking classes, I can resist everything except temptations, etc. 258pp. 5⅜ × 8½. (USCO)
20602-5 Pa. $3.50

THE DEVIL'S DICTIONARY, Ambrose Bierce. Barbed, bitter, brilliant witticisms in the form of a dictionary. Best, most ferocious satire America has produced. 145pp. 5⅜ × 8½.   20487-1 Pa. $2.50

ERTÉ'S FASHION DESIGNS, Erté. 210 black-and-white inventions from *Harper's Bazar*, 1918-32, plus 8pp. full-color covers. Captions. 88pp. 9 × 12.
24203-X Pa. $6.50

ERTÉ GRAPHICS, Erté. Collection of striking color graphics: *Seasons, Alphabet, Numerals, Aces* and *Precious Stones*. 50 plates, including 4 on covers. 48pp. 9⅜ × 12¼.   23580-7 Pa. $6.95

PAPER FOLDING FOR BEGINNERS, William D. Murray and Francis J. Rigney. Clearest book for making origami sail boats, roosters, frogs that move legs, etc. 40 projects. More than 275 illustrations. 94pp. 5⅜ × 8½.   20713-7 Pa. $2.25

ORIGAMI FOR THE ENTHUSIAST, John Montroll. Fish, ostrich, peacock, squirrel, rhinoceros, Pegasus, 19 other intricate subjects. Instructions. Diagrams. 128pp. 9 × 12.   23799-0 Pa. $4.95

CROCHETING NOVELTY POT HOLDERS, edited by Linda Macho. 64 useful, whimsical pot holders feature kitchen themes, animals, flowers, other novelties. Surprisingly easy to crochet. Complete instructions. 48pp. 8¼ × 11.
24296-X Pa. $1.95

CROCHETING DOILIES, edited by Rita Weiss. Irish Crochet, Jewel, Star Wheel, Vanity Fair and more. Also luncheon and console sets, runners and centerpieces. 51 illustrations. 48pp. 8¼ × 11.   23424-X Pa. $2.00

YUCATAN BEFORE AND AFTER THE CONQUEST, Diego de Landa. Only significant account of Yucatan written in the early post-Conquest era. Translated by William Gates. Over 120 illustrations. 162pp. 5⅜ × 8½. 23622-6 Pa. $3.50

ORNATE PICTORIAL CALLIGRAPHY, E.A. Lupfer. Complete instructions, over 150 examples help you create magnificent "flourishes" from which beautiful animals and objects gracefully emerge. 8⅛ × 11. 21957-7 Pa. $2.95

DOLLY DINGLE PAPER DOLLS, Grace Drayton. Cute chubby children by same artist who did Campbell Kids. Rare plates from 1910s. 30 paper dolls and over 100 outfits reproduced in full color. 32pp. 9¼ × 12¼. 23711-7 Pa. $3.50

CURIOUS GEORGE PAPER DOLLS IN FULL COLOR, H. A. Rey, Kathy Allert. Naughty little monkey-hero of children's books in two doll figures, plus 48 full-color costumes: pirate, Indian chief, fireman, more. 32pp. 9¼ × 12¼. 24386-9 Pa. $3.50

GERMAN: HOW TO SPEAK AND WRITE IT, Joseph Rosenberg. Like *French, How to Speak and Write It.* Very rich modern course, with a wealth of pictorial material. 330 illustrations. 384pp. 5⅜ × 8½. (USUKO) 20271-2 Pa. $4.75

CATS AND KITTENS: 24 Ready-to-Mail Color Photo Postcards, D. Holby. Handsome collection; feline in a variety of adorable poses. Identifications. 12pp. on postcard stock. 8¼ × 11. 24469-5 Pa. $2.95

MARILYN MONROE PAPER DOLLS, Tom Tierney. 31 full-color designs on heavy stock, from *The Asphalt Jungle, Gentlemen Prefer Blondes,* 22 others. 1 doll. 16 plates. 32pp. 9⅜ × 12¼. 23769-9 Pa. $3.50

FUNDAMENTALS OF LAYOUT, F.H. Wills. All phases of layout design discussed and illustrated in 121 illustrations. Indispensable as student's text or handbook for professional. 124pp. 8⅛ × 11. 21279-3 Pa. $4.50

FANTASTIC SUPER STICKERS, Ed Sibbett, Jr. 75 colorful pressure-sensitive stickers. Peel off and place for a touch of pizzazz: clowns, penguins, teddy bears, etc. Full color. 16pp. 8¼ × 11. 24471-7 Pa. $2.95

LABELS FOR ALL OCCASIONS, Ed Sibbett, Jr. 6 labels each of 16 different designs—baroque, art nouveau, art deco, Pennsylvania Dutch, etc.—in full color. 24pp. 8¼ × 11. 23688-9 Pa. $2.95

HOW TO CALCULATE QUICKLY: RAPID METHODS IN BASIC MATHEMATICS, Henry Sticker. Addition, subtraction, multiplication, division, checks, etc. More than 8000 problems, solutions. 185pp. 5 × 7¼. 20295-X Pa. $2.95

THE CAT COLORING BOOK, Karen Baldauski. Handsome, realistic renderings of 40 splendid felines, from American shorthair to exotic types. 44 plates. Captions. 48pp. 8¼ × 11. 24011-8 Pa. $2.25

THE TALE OF PETER RABBIT, Beatrix Potter. The inimitable Peter's terrifying adventure in Mr. McGregor's garden, with all 27 wonderful, full-color Potter illustrations. 55pp. 4¼ × 5½. (Available in U.S. only) 22827-4 Pa. $1.60

BASIC ELECTRICITY, U.S. Bureau of Naval Personnel. Batteries, circuits, conductors, AC and DC, inductance and capacitance, generators, motors, transformers, amplifiers, etc. 349 illustrations. 448pp. 6½ × 9¼. 20973-3 Pa. $7.95

SOURCE BOOK OF MEDICAL HISTORY, edited by Logan Clendening, M.D. Original accounts ranging from Ancient Egypt and Greece to discovery of X-rays: Galen, Pasteur, Lavoisier, Harvey, Parkinson, others. 685pp. 5⅜ × 8½.
20621-1 Pa. $10.95

THE ROSE AND THE KEY, J.S. Lefanu. Superb mystery novel from Irish master. Dark doings among an ancient and aristocratic English family. Well-drawn characters; capital suspense. Introduction by N. Donaldson. 448pp. 5⅜ × 8½.
24377-X Pa. $6.95

SOUTH WIND, Norman Douglas. Witty, elegant novel of ideas set on languorous Mediterranean island of Nepenthe. Elegant prose, glittering epigrams, mordant satire. 1917 masterpiece. 416pp. 5⅜ × 8½. (Available in U.S. only)
24361-3 Pa. $5.95

RUSSELL'S CIVIL WAR PHOTOGRAPHS, Capt. A.J. Russell. 116 rare Civil War Photos: Bull Run, Virginia campaigns, bridges, railroads, Richmond, Lincoln's funeral car. Many never seen before. Captions. 128pp. 9⅜ × 12¼.
24283-8 Pa. $6.95

PHOTOGRAPHS BY MAN RAY: 105 Works, 1920-1934. Nudes, still lifes, landscapes, women's faces, celebrity portraits (Dali, Matisse, Picasso, others), rayographs. Reprinted from rare gravure edition. 128pp. 9⅜ × 12¼. (Available in U.S. only)
23842-3 Pa. $6.95

STAR NAMES: THEIR LORE AND MEANING, Richard H. Allen. Star names, the zodiac, constellations: folklore and literature associated with heavens. The basic book of its field, fascinating reading. 563pp. 5⅜ × 8½.
21079-0 Pa. $7.95

BURNHAM'S CELESTIAL HANDBOOK, Robert Burnham, Jr. Thorough guide to the stars beyond our solar system. Exhaustive treatment. Alphabetical by constellation: Andromeda to Cetus in Vol. 1; Chamaeleon to Orion in Vol. 2; and Pavo to Vulpecula in Vol. 3. Hundreds of illustrations. Index in Vol. 3. 2000pp. 6⅛ × 9¼.
23567-X, 23568-8, 23673-0 Pa. Three-vol. set $36.85

THE ART NOUVEAU STYLE BOOK OF ALPHONSE MUCHA, Alphonse Mucha. All 72 plates from *Documents Decoratifs* in original color. Stunning, essential work of Art Nouveau. 80pp. 9⅜ × 12¼.
24044-4 Pa. $7.95

DESIGNS BY ERTE; FASHION DRAWINGS AND ILLUSTRATIONS FROM "HARPER'S BAZAR," Erte. 310 fabulous line drawings and 14 *Harper's Bazar* covers, 8 in full color. Erte's exotic temptresses with tassels, fur muffs, long trains, coifs, more. 129pp. 9⅜ × 12¼.
23397-9 Pa. $6.95

HISTORY OF STRENGTH OF MATERIALS, Stephen P. Timoshenko. Excellent historical survey of the strength of materials with many references to the theories of elasticity and structure. 245 figures. 452pp. 5⅜ × 8½. 61187-6 Pa. $8.95

Prices subject to change without notice.

Available at your book dealer or write for free catalog to Dept. GI, Dover Publications, Inc., 31 East 2nd St. Mineola, N.Y. 11501. Dover publishes more than 175 books each year on science, elementary and advanced mathematics, biology, music, art, literary history, social sciences and other areas.